The Student Promise Pocketbook

Harold Shaw Publishers
Wheaton, Illinois

Grateful acknowledgment is made to the publishers of the Scripture versions, portions of which are quoted in this book, using the following abbreviations:

KJV   *The King James Version*
NASB   *The New American Standard Bible*
NIV   *The New International Version*
Phillips *The New Testament In Modern English*
         by J. B. Phillips
RSV   *The Revised Standard Version*
TEV   *Today's English Version (Good News Bible)*
TLB   *The Living Bible*

The New American Standard Bible, Copyright © 1960, 1962, 1963, 1968, 1971, 1972, 1973, 1975, 1977 by the Lockman Foundation. Used by permission.
The Holy Bible, New International Version, Copyright © 1978 by New York International Bible Society. Used by permission of Zondervan Bible Publishers.
The New Testament in Modern English, revised edition by J.B. Phillips, Copyright © 1958, 1960, 1972, by J.B. Phillips. Used by permission of the Macmillan Publishing Company, Inc.
The Revised Standard Version of the Bible, Copyright © 1946, 1952, 1971, 1973. Used by permission.
Scripture quotations from TEV are from the *Good News Bible, The Bible in Today's English Version.* Copyright © 1976 by the American Bible Society. Used by permission.
The Living Bible, Copyright © 1971 by Tyndale House Publishers, Wheaton, Illinois. Used by permission.

Copyright © 1982 by Harold Shaw Publishers

The Student Promise Pocketbook is compiled and edited by Ann Alexander and Fay Blix.

ISBN 0-87788-912-0

Printed in Colombia.
Impreso en Colombia.

99 98

21 20

How To Use Your Promise Book: The Four-Way System

"This God—his way is perfect; the promise of the Lord proves true." (Psalm 18:30)

God's Word, the Bible, is full of promises—promises made to his children whom he loves. Because God is God, and his very nature is truth, he cannot be unfaithful to these promises or his purposes. Everything that he has guaranteed to each of us, we can trust him to carry out completely.

As you use this *Student Promise Pocketbook*, remember that these verses are God's guarantees to you, his child. Through prayer and practice, these promises can become part of your life, giving you hope, joy and victory.

Step One:
Ask yourself, "In what area of my life do I need to hear God's Word? What are my feelings right now? What are my struggles?" Look at the four sections of the index, which starts on page 7—*My Relationship with God, Living with Myself, Living with My Family and Others,* and *My Life at School.* Now turn to the section that *asks your question,* that fits your present situation. Read the verses slowly, carefully, letting his Word fill your heart and mind.

Step Two:

Choose one of the verses which speaks to you, that touches you and check the first box next to that promise. Then write today's date in the space provided. Claim this verse as God's guarantee to you today! Know that he has given it to you! (You may want to look it up in your Bible and read it in its context.)

Step Three:

Copy the verse on a notecard so that you can keep it with you, and memorize it. Memorizing comes quickly and easily when you read the verse several times a day. Tape it to the dashboard of your car, your school notebook, your bathroom mirror, your desk or bulletin board —wherever you're sure to see it often and claim it as your own.

Step Four:

Turn to the prayer page at the end of the book or use the reverse side of your memory card and write a short prayer to God thanking Him for his promise to you (state it specifically in terms of your situation) and claim the promise for your own life.

Applying the Four-Way System

Here are some illustrations of how the Promise Book may be used.

Another member of your school basketball team has made some nasty comments about your game skills. To make things worse, this person is the only other Christian on the team! God's promise to you in this situation might be one found on page 78 of this Promise Book:

Be humble and gentle. Be patient with each other,

making allowance for each other's faults because of
your love. Try always to be led along together by the
Holy Spirit, and so be at peace with one another.
Ephesians 4:2, 3 (TLB).

Here's a prayer you could write: "Lord, I forgive Sandy
for those cutting remarks. Make me more loving and co-
operative. Help me to be a good team-mate and a better
player. Join Sandy's spirit and mine in your love so that
we can show others how well Christians get along. In
Jesus' name. Amen."

Or, perhaps you have been anxious because of an
urgent financial need, or bad health. You might find that
this promise on page 55 speaks to you:

My God, with all his abundant wealth in Christ Jesus,
will supply all your needs. *Philippians 4:19 (TEV).*

Then you may record a prayer like this: "Lord, I choose
not to panic in this emergency. You know how much
tuition costs and you know the amount in my bank
account. Because you love me, I believe you will not only
supply the funds but keep me calm until the bill is paid.
Thank you, Jesus, my Lord, Amen."

Or, you may feel that God is far away. You're miser-
able about your emptiness and lack of joy in God. This
verse on page 30 may be the promise for you:

Be humble then before God. But resist the devil and
you'll find he'll run away from you. Come close to God
and he will come close to you. You are sinners: get
your hands clean again. Your loyalty is divided: get
your hearts made true once more. You must humble
yourselves in the sight of the Lord before he will lift you
up. *James 4:7, 8, 10 (Phillips)*

If your heart responds to these words, your prayer may
be: "Lord, make me humble before you. I realize now
that I have turned away from you. Give me clean hands
and a true heart and help me always to run away from
the devil and toward you. In Jesus' name. Amen."

6

Finally

As God's promise becomes reality and you recognize the fulfillment of his Word to you, check the second box and fill in the date. And remember, if God's promises are true now, they will prove true tomorrow and he will continue to carry them out again and again for the rest of your life!

Your Index To God's Promises & Purposes

• Things are so impersonal at school. How can I be sure I'm not just a number to God?   *34*

Section 2:
Living with Myself

• I'm even a stranger to myself these days. Does God know who I really am?   *35*

• I don't know what to do with my life. Does God have dreams and plans for me?   *36*

• I feel like a walking disaster area. How can God still love me when I keep fouling things up?   *36*

• Everything I do is such a pale imitation of what I meant to do. Is God disappointed in me, too?   *37*

• I feel as though life has given me a dirty rotten deal. Will God help me overcome my bitterness?   *38*

• Nothing makes much sense to me anymore. How can I discover meaning in life?   *39*

• Sometimes I feel as though I simply cannot go on living. Where can I find reasons to keep hanging on?   *39*

• I'm afraid I'm going to go crazy. Will God help me hold my pieces together?   *40*

• Most days I feel as tense as a taut rubber band. Can I count on God to keep me from snapping apart?   *41*

• I feel so inferior to almost everyone. How do I rate in God's eyes?   *42*

• I cry easily. Does God understand why?   *42*

• There are times when I get so angry I feel like throwing and smashing things. How does God want me to respond when I feel angry?   *43*

• I get depressed every time I look in the mirror. How does God see me?   *44*

• I often feel panic when I think about the future. Where can I turn for help and reassurance?   *45*

Section 3:
Living with My Family and Others

• My parents are always fighting. I'm afraid they are going to get a divorce. What do I have to hold on to? 59

• My parents simply don't understand me. Can God help us to communicate? 59

• My parents are divorced and I'm caught in the middle. Can God help me deal with this situation without being torn apart? 60

• My father rarely was around while I was growing up, so I've never really known what it's like to have a father. Will God be a father to me? 61

• My mother is terminally ill. How can God help us to cope? 61

• Someone I really loved has just been killed in a car accident. Will God help me out of my depression? 62

• My parents, boss and teachers nag me continually. How does God want me to respond to authorities in my life? 63

• My family isn't Christian and they ridicule my faith and laugh when I talk about God. How should I relate to them? 64

• My desire to follow Jesus causes friction and division between me and my skeptical family. Is this really God's will? 65

• I'm adopted and my parents treat me differently from their natural children. Will God consider me as one of his true children? 65

• I'm so lonely and homesick I feel as if I'm going to die. Does God understand how I feel? 66

• I often argue and disagree with my brothers and sisters. Can God help my relationships with them? 66

- I want to share my faith with others. How can I be more than a "witless witness"? *79*

- I get enraged at bigots. Can God keep me from being bigotted about bigots? *80*

- Many people have less than I do, but if I give to them, how will I have enough left for myself? *80*

Section 4:
My Life at School

- I wanted to do so well this term and I've already blown the first test. Can God give me the energy to keep trying? *82*

- I just received a D on my test and I'm really hurting. How do I measure up in God's eyes? *82*

- I'm so busy and there are so many demands on my time, I don't even have time to think. How can I slow down? *83*

- Some of my teachers are sarcastic and critical of my performance. Is God critical and judgmental too? *84*

- I wish I could drop out of school. Would God love me even if I were a dropout? *85*

- It's scary to be out on my own for the first time. How can I be sure that God is still with me? *85*

- I feel so stupid and thick-brained. Does God really love slow people and underachievers like me? *86*

- I'm terrified of flunking out of school. How can I deal with my anxiety? *87*

- I got straight A's this semester. How can God help me to keep my priorities straight and keep me from pride? *87*

- The person who sits next to me cheats in every exam and then gets A's. Will God help me to avoid being bitter about this situation? *88*

My Relationship with God

___

I've had so much religion crammed down my throat that sometimes God seems just a cliché to me. How can God be real in my life?

1. Come close to God and he will come close to you. *James 4:8 (Phillips)*
□_____ □_____

2. Jesus replied, "If anyone loves me, he will obey my teaching. My Father will love him, and we will come to him and make our home with him." *John 14:23 (NIV)*
□_____ □_____

3. The man who does obey God's commands lives in God and God lives in him, and the guarantee of his presence within us is the Spirit he has given us. *1 John 3:24 (Phillips)* □_____ □_____

4. But to all who received [Jesus], who believed in his name, he gave power to become children of God; who were born, not of blood nor of the will of the flesh nor of the will of man, but of God. *John 1:12-13 (RSV)*
□_____ □_____

5. Jesus shouted to the crowds, "If you trust me, you are really trusting God. For when you see me, you are seeing the one who sent me." *John 12:44-45 (TLB)*
□_____ □_____

When I pray it feels as if I'm just talking to myself. Is God really listening to my prayers?

1. We have courage in God's presence because we are

sure that he hears us if we ask him for anything that is according to his will. He hears us whenever we ask him; since we know this is true, we know also that he gives us what we ask from him. *1 John 5:14–15 (TEV)*

☐_____ ☐_____

2. Then you will call upon me and come and pray to me, and I will listen to you. You will seek me and find me when you seek me with all your heart. I will be found by you, declares the Lord. *Jeremiah 29:12–14 (NIV)*

☐_____ ☐_____

3. Even before they finish praying to me, I will answer their prayers. *Isaiah 65:24 (TEV)*

☐_____ ☐_____

4. The righteous call to the Lord, and he listens; he rescues them from all their troubles. *Psalm 34:17 (TEV)*

☐_____ ☐_____

5. For we do not know how we ought to pray; the Spirit himself pleads with God for us, in groans that words cannot express. And God, who sees into the hearts of men, knows what the thought of the Spirit is; because the Spirit pleads with God on behalf of his people and in accordance with his will. *Romans 8:26–27 (TEV)*

☐_____ ☐_____

6. Whatever we ask we receive from Him, because we keep His commandments and do the things that are pleasing in His sight. And this is His commandment, that we believe in the name of His Son Jesus Christ, and love one another, just as He commanded us. *1 John 3:22–23 (NASB)* ☐_____ ☐_____

I feel so sad about all the people who are hurting in the world. Does God really care about suffering people?

1. But you do see; you take notice of trouble and suffering and are always ready to help. The helpless man commits himself to you; you have always helped the needy. *Psalm 10:14 (TEV)*

☐_____ ☐_____

2. For he has not despised or disdained the suffering of the afflicted one; he has not hidden his face from him but has listened to his cry for help. *Psalm 22:24 (NIV)*

☐_____ ☐_____

3. You hear, O Lord, the desire of the afflicted; you encourage them, and you listen to their cry, defending the fatherless and the oppressed, in order that man, who is of the earth, may terrify no more. *Psalm 10:17-18 (NIV)* ☐_____ ☐_____

4. For God loved the world so much that he gave his only Son, so that everyone who believes in him should not be lost, but should have eternal life. God has not sent his Son into the world to pass sentence on it, but to save it—through him. *John 3:16-17 (Phillips)*

☐_____ ☐_____

5. And yet the Lord is waiting to be merciful to you. He is ready to take pity on you because he always does what is right. Happy are those who put their trust in the Lord. *Isaiah 30:18 (TEV)* ☐_____ ☐_____

I'm really upset by some of the horrible things that people have done in the name of Christianity. Is God really good?

1. I will praise the name of the Lord, and his people will tell of his greatness. The Lord is your mighty defender, perfect and just in all his ways; Your God is faithful and true; he does what is right and fair. *Deuteronomy 32:3-4 (TEV)* ☐_____ ☐_____

2. For the Lord is always good. He is always loving and

kind, and his faithfulness goes on and on to each suc-
ceeding generation. *Psalm 100:5 (TLB)*

□_____ □_____

3. The law of the Lord is perfect; it gives new strength.
The commands of the Lord are trustworthy, giving wis-
dom to those who lack it. The laws of the Lord are right,
and those who obey them are happy. The commands of
the Lord are just and give understanding to the mind.
The worship of the Lord is good; it will continue forever.
The judgments of the Lord are just; they are always fair.
Psalm 19:7-9 (TEV) □

4. I will sing of thy steadfast love, O Lord, for ever; with
my mouth I will proclaim thy faithfulness to all generations. For thy steadfast love was established for ever, thy
faithfulness is firm as the heavens. *Psalm 89:1-2 (RSV)*

□_____ □_____

*Whenever I start reading my Bible, I get
bored and frustrated. It just doesn't speak
to me. Does God really have anything to
say to me in his book?*

1. For all those words which were written long ago are
meant to teach us today; so that we may be encouraged
to endure and to go on hoping in our own time. *Romans
15:4 (Phillips)* □_____ □_____

2. All Scripture is God-breathed and is useful for teaching, rebuking, correcting and training in righteousness,
so that the man of God may be thoroughly equipped for
every good work. *2 Timothy 3:16-17 (NIV)*

□_____ □_____

3. Thy word is a lamp to my feet and a light to my path.
The unfolding of thy words gives light; it imparts understanding to the simple. *Psalm 119:105, 130 (RSV)*

□_____ □_____

4. Your words are what sustain me; they are good to my hungry soul. They bring joy to my sorrowing heart and delight me. *Jeremiah 15:16 (TLB)*

☐ _____ ☐ _____

5. Man cannot live on bread alone, but on every word that God speaks. *Matthew 4:4 (TEV)*

☐ _____ ☐ _____

6. This book of the law shall not depart from your mouth, but you shall meditate on it day and night, so that you may be careful to do according to all that is written in it; for then you will make your way prosperous, and then you will have success. *Joshua 1:8 (NASB)*

☐ _____ ☐ _____

Some of my teachers tell me that the Bible is just myths. How can I know for sure that it truly is God's Word?

1. All scripture is inspired by God and is useful for teaching the faith and correcting error, for resetting the direction of a man's life and training him in good living. *2 Timothy 3:16 (Phillips)*

☐ _____ ☐ _____

2. For no prophecy recorded in Scripture was ever thought up by the prophet himself. It was the Holy Spirit within these godly men who gave them true messages from God. *2 Peter 1:20–21 (TLB)*

☐ _____ ☐ _____

3. Jesus answered, "My teaching is not my own. It comes from him who sent me. If a man chooses to do God's will, he will find out whether my teaching comes from God or whether I speak on my own." *John 7:16–17 (NIV)* ☐ _____ ☐ _____

It seems as though the world is pretty messed up in spite of God's existence. Can I trust his presence and protection in my life?

1. Though I walk in the midst of trouble, you preserve my life; you stretch out your hand against the anger of my foes, with your right hand you save me. The Lord will fulfill his purpose for me; your love, O Lord, endures forever—do not abandon the works of your hands. *Psalm 138:7-8 (NIV)*

☐_____   ☐_____

2. The Lord will guard you; he is by your side to protect you. The sun will not hurt you during the day, nor the moon during the night. The Lord will protect you from all danger; he will keep you safe. He will protect you as you come and go now and forever. *Psalm 121:5-8 (TEV)*

☐_____   ☐_____

3. If I take the wings of the morning and dwell in the uttermost parts of the sea, even there thy hand shall lead me, and thy right hand shall hold me. *Psalm 139:9-10 (RSV)* ☐_____   ☐_____

4. "I am the Lord, the God of all mankind. Is anything too hard for me?" Ah, Sovereign Lord, you have made the heavens and the earth by your great power and outstretched arm. Nothing is too hard for you. *Jeremiah 32:27, 17 (NIV)* ☐_____   ☐_____

5. But the Lord is still in his holy temple; he still rules from heaven. He closely watches everything that happens here on earth. He puts the righteous and the wicked to the test; he hates those loving violence. For God is good, and he loves goodness; the godly shall see his face. *Psalm 11:4-5, 7 (TLB)*

☐_____   ☐_____

6. Those who trust in the Lord are like Mount Zion, which cannot be shaken but endures forever. As the mountains surround Jerusalem, so the Lord surrounds his people both now and forevermore. *Psalm 125:1-2 (NIV)* ☐ _____ ☐ _____

Intellectually I know God has forgiven me, but I don't feel forgiven or live as if I'm forgiven. How do I really know that he has forgiven me?

1. If we confess our sins, he is faithful and just to forgive us our sins, and to cleanse us from all unrighteousness. *1 John 1:9 (KJV)*

☐ _____ ☐ _____

2. And yet, I am the God who forgives your sins, and I do this because of who I am. I will not hold your sins against you. *Isaiah 43:25 (TEV)*

☐ _____ ☐ _____

3. He saved us—not because we were good enough to be saved, but because of his kindness and pity—by washing away our sins and giving us the new joy of the indwelling Holy Spirit. *Titus 3:5 (TLB)*

☐ _____ ☐ _____

4. He does not punish us as we deserve or repay us for our sins and wrongs. As high as the sky is above the earth, so great is his love for those who have reverence for him. As far as the east is from the west, so far does he remove our sins from us. *Psalm 103:10-12 (TEV)*

☐ _____ ☐ _____

5. He rescued us from the power of darkness and brought us safe into the kingdom of his dear Son, by whom we are set free, that is, our sins are forgiven. *Colossians 1:13-14 (TEV)*

☐ _____ ☐ _____

My faith has been shaken by some of the things I've been learning in class. Will God write me off during periods of doubt?

1. Even when we are too weak to have any faith left, he remains faithful to us and will help us, for he cannot disown us who are part of himself, and he will always carry out his promises to us. *2 Timothy 2:13 (TLB)*

☐_____ ☐_____

2. Because of his kindness you have been saved through trusting Christ. And even trusting is not of yourselves; it too is a gift from God. *Ephesians 2:8 (TLB)*

☐_____ ☐_____

3. As a father has compassion on his children, so the Lord has compassion on those who fear him; for he knows how we are formed, he remembers that we are dust. *Psalm 103:13–14 (NIV)*

☐_____ ☐_____

4. You will seek me and find me; when you seek me with all your heart, I will be found by you, says the Lord. *Jeremiah 29:13–14 (RSV)*

☐_____ ☐_____

5. He is patient with you, not wanting anyone to perish, but everyone to come to repentance. *2 Peter 3:9 (NIV)*

☐_____ ☐_____

6. Nothing can separate us from his love: neither death nor life; neither angels nor other heavenly rulers or powers; neither the present nor the future; neither the world above nor the world below—there is nothing in all creation that will ever be able to separate us from the love of God which is ours through Christ Jesus our Lord. *Romans 8:38–39 (TEV)*

☐_____ ☐_____

7. Return to me and I will return to you, says the Lord of hosts. *Malachi 3:7 (RSV)*

☐_____ ☐_____

People have so many different ideas about God. Can I trust God to give me true understanding about himself?

1. And I will lead the blind by a way they do not know, in paths they do not know I will guide them. I will make darkness into light before them and rugged places into plains. These are the things I will do, and I will not leave them undone. *Isaiah 42:16 (NASB)*

☐＿＿＿＿＿ ☐＿＿＿＿＿

2. Jesus said, "If you hold to my teaching, you are really my disciples. Then you will know the truth, and the truth will set you free." *John 8:31-32 (NIV)*

☐＿＿＿＿＿ ☐＿＿＿＿＿

3. When the Spirit of truth comes, he will guide you into all the truth; for he will not speak on his own authority, but whatever he hears he will speak, and he will declare to you the things that are to come. *John 16:13 (RSV)*

☐＿＿＿＿＿ ☐＿＿＿＿＿

4. He reveals things that are deep and secret; he knows what is hidden in darkness, and he himself is surrounded by light. *Daniel 2:22 (TEV)*

☐＿＿＿＿＿ ☐＿＿＿＿＿

5. You guide me with your instruction and at the end you will receive me with honor. *Psalm 73:24 (TEV)*

☐＿＿＿＿＿ ☐＿＿＿＿＿

6. Then he opened their minds so they could understand the Scriptures. *Luke 24:45 (NIV)*

☐＿＿＿＿＿ ☐＿＿＿＿＿

I know God created this huge world, but how can I be sure that he cares for me— one person among billions?

1. I will be your God through all your lifetime, yes, even when your hair is white with age. I made you and I will care for you. I will carry you along and be your Savior. *Isaiah 46:4 (TLB)* □_____ □_____

2. It is God himself who makes us sure, with you, of our life in Christ; it is God himself who has set us apart, who placed his mark of ownership upon us, and who gave the Holy Spirit in our hearts as the guarantee of all that he has for us. *2 Corinthians 1:21–22 (TEV)*

□_____ □_____

3. Israel, the Lord who created you says, "Do not be afraid—I will save you. I have called you by name—you are mine." *Isaiah 43:1 (TEV)*

□_____ □_____

4. But even the very hairs of your head are all numbered. Fear not therefore: ye are of more value than many sparrows. *Luke 12:7 (KJV)*

□_____ □_____

5. He found him in a desert land, and in the howling waste of the wilderness; he encircled him, he cared for him, he kept him as the apple of his eye. *Deuteronomy 32:10 (RSV)* □_____ □_____

Life is so confusing—the more I learn, the more I discover grey areas instead of blacks and whites. Will God help me to be discerning?

1. If any of you does not know how to meet any particular problem he has only to ask God—who gives generously to all men without making them feel guilty—and he may be quite sure that the necessary wisdom will be given him. *James 1:5 (Phillips)*

□_____ □_____

2. He guides the humble in what is right and teaches them his way. *Psalm 25:9 (NIV)*

□_____ □_____

3. The Lord will make you go through hard times, but he himself will be there to teach you, and you will not have to search for him any more. If you wander off the road to the right or the left, you will hear his voice behind you saying, "Here is the road. Follow it." *Isaiah 30:20–21 (TEV)* □_____ □_____

4. But the Counselor, the Holy Spirit, whom the Father will send in my name, will teach you all things and will remind you of everything I have said to you. *John 14:26 (NIV)* □_____ □_____

5. When the Spirit of truth comes, he will guide you into all the truth; for he will not speak on his own authority, but whatever he hears he will speak. *John 16:13 (RSV)* □_____ □_____

My behavior always lags behind my convictions. Can God help me stand up for what I believe?

1. Give yourself to the Lord; trust in him, and he will help you; he will make your righteousness shine like the noonday sun. *Psalm 37:5-6 (TEV)* □_____ □_____

2. Now unto him that is able to keep you from falling, and to present you faultless before the presence of his glory with exceeding joy, to the only wise God our Saviour, be glory and majesty, dominion and power, both now and ever. Amen. *Jude 1:24–25 (KJV)* □_____ □_____

3. God is always at work in you to make you willing and able to obey his own purpose. *Philippians 2:13 (TEV)* □_____ □_____

have drawn you with lovingkindness. *Jeremiah 31:3 (NASB)* ☐_____ ☐_____

3. But God has shown us how much he loves us; it was while we were still sinners that Christ died for us! *Romans 5:8 (TEV)*

☐_____ ☐_____

4. Consider the incredible love that the Father has shown us in allowing us to be called "children of God"— and that is not just what we are called, but what we *are*. *1 John 3:1 (Phillips)*

☐_____ ☐_____

5. The Lord is merciful and loving, slow to become angry and full of constant love. *Psalm 103:8 (TEV)*

☐_____ ☐_____

6. This is what love is: it is not that we have loved God, but that he loved us and sent his Son to be the means by which our sins are forgiven. *1 John 4:10 (TEV)*

☐_____ ☐_____

My whole life seems to be falling apart— everything is changing. Can I count on God to be the stabilizing force in my life?

1. For this God is our God for ever and ever; he will be our guide even to the end. *Psalm 48:14 (NIV)*

☐_____ ☐_____

2. Remember that the Lord your God is the only God and that he is faithful. He will keep his covenant and show his constant love to a thousand generations of those who love him and obey his commands. *Deuteronomy 7:9 (TEV)* ☐_____ ☐_____

3. Jesus Christ is always the same, yesterday, today and for ever. *Hebrews 13:8 (Phillips)*

☐_____ ☐_____

4. Before you created the hills or brought the world into being, you were eternally God, and will be God forever. *Psalm 90:2 (TEV)* ☐ _____ ☐ _____

5. For I, the Lord, do not change. *Malachi 3:6 (NASB)* ☐ _____ ☐ _____

Nothing seems easy. Why did God make life such a constant struggle?

1. When all kinds of trials and temptations crowd into your lives, my brothers, don't resent them as intruders, but welcome them as friends! Realize that they come to test your faith and to produce in you the quality of endurance. But let the process go on until that endurance is fully developed, and you will find you have become men of mature character, men of integrity with no weak spots. *James 1:3–4 (Phillips)* ☐ _____ ☐ _____

2. But God disciplines us for our good, that we may share in his holiness. No discipline seems pleasant at the time, but painful. Later on, however, it produces a harvest of righteousness and peace for those who have been trained by it. *Hebrews 12:10–11 (NIV)* ☐ _____ ☐ _____

3. My son, do not make light of the Lord's discipline, and do not lose heart when he rebukes you, because the Lord disciplines those whom he loves, and he punishes everyone he accepts as a son. *Hebrews 12:5–6 (NIV)* ☐ _____ ☐ _____

4. My dear friends, do not be surprised at the painful test you are suffering, as though something unusual were happening to you. Rather be glad that you are sharing Christ's sufferings, so that you may be full of joy when his glory is revealed. *1 Peter 4:12–13 (TEV)* ☐ _____ ☐ _____

5. Blessed are you who are poor, for yours is the kingdom of God. Blessed are you who hunger now, for you will be satisfied. Blessed are you who weep now, for you will laugh. Blessed are you when men hate you, when they exclude you and insult you and reject your name as evil, because of the Son of Man. Rejoice in that day and leap for joy, because great is your reward in heaven. *Luke 6:20–23 (NIV)*

☐_____ ☐_____

My Christian family really supports me in my faith; but when I'm not with them, I feel so alone. Can I stay close to God without their help?

1. I am not going to leave you alone in the world—I am coming to you. *John 14:18 (Phillips)*

☐_____ ☐_____

2. The Lord your God is with you; his power gives you victory. The Lord will take delight in you, and in his love he will give you new life. He will sing and be joyful over you. *Zephaniah 3:17 (TEV)*

☐_____ ☐_____

3. And behold I am with you, and will keep you wherever you go, for I will not leave you until I have done what I have promised you. *Genesis 28:15 (NASB)*

☐_____ ☐_____

4. Be strong and courageous. Do not be afraid or terrified because of them, for the Lord your God goes with you; he will never leave you nor forsake you. *Deuteronomy 31:6 (NIV)* ☐_____ ☐_____

5. When you pray, I will answer you. When you call to me, I will respond. *Isaiah 58:9 (TEV)*

☐_____ ☐_____

30

School is so overwhelming that I haven't been able to spend any decent time with God lately. How will this affect my standing with him?

1. My sheep hear my voice, and I know them, and they follow me: and I give unto them eternal life; and they shall never perish, neither shall any man pluck them out of my hand. *John 10:27–28 (KJV)*
☐_____ ☐_____

2. Fear not, for I am with you, be not dismayed, for I am your God; I will strengthen you, I will help you, I will uphold you with my victorious right hand. *Isaiah 41:10 (RSV)* ☐_____ ☐_____

3. Obey my voice, and I will be your God, and you shall be my people; and walk in all the way that I command you, that it may be well with you. *Jeremiah 7:23 (RSV)*
☐_____ ☐_____

4. How happy are those who hear the word of God and obey! *Luke 11:28 (TEV)*

God seems very far away. How can I get in touch with him again?

1. If my people who are called by my name humble themselves, and pray and seek my face, and turn from their wicked ways, then I will hear from heaven, and will forgive their sin and heal their land. *2 Chronicles 7:14 (RSV)* ☐_____ ☐_____

2. Be humble then before God. But resist the devil and you'll find he'll run away from you. Come close to God and he will come close to you. You are sinners: get your hands clean again. Your loyalty is divided: get your hearts made true once more. You must humble your-

selves in the sight of the Lord before he will lift you up.
James 4:7, 8, 10 (Phillips)
□_____ □_____

3. I will pray morning, noon, and night, pleading aloud with God; and he will hear and answer. *Psalm 55:17 (TLB)* □_____ □_____

4. No one has ever seen God; but if we love each other, God lives in us and his love is made complete in us. *1 John 4:12 (NIV)* □_____ □_____

5. Ask, and it shall be given you; seek, and ye shall find; knock, and it shall be opened unto you. *Matthew 7:7 (KJV)* □_____ □_____

Sometimes church strikes me as rigid and ritualistic. How can I worship God in a way that really pleases him?

1. I don't want your sacrifices—I want your love; I don't want your offerings—I want you to know me. *Hosea 6:6 (TLB)* □_____ □_____

2. The sacrifice acceptable to God is a broken spirit; a broken and contrite heart, O God, thou wilt not despise. *Psalm 51:17 (RSV)*
□_____ □_____

3. What does the Lord your God require of you, but to fear the Lord your God, to walk in all his ways, to love him, to serve the Lord your God with all your heart and with all your soul, and to keep the commandments and statutes of the Lord, for your good. *Deuteronomy 10:12-13 (RSV)* □_____ □_____

4. The Lord has told us what is good. What he requires of us is this: to do what is just, to show constant love, and to live in humble fellowship with our God. *Micah 6:8 (TEV)* □_____ □_____

5. But the hour is coming, and now is, when the true

worshipers will worship the Father in spirit and truth, for such the Father seeks to worship him. God is spirit, and those who worship him must worship in spirit and truth. *John 4:23–24 (RSV)*

□ _____ □ _____

Everyone is so busy around here that unless there is something seriously wrong, I hate to bother anyone. Does God mind my calling on him even if I don't have an emergency?

1. Just as you trusted Christ to save you, trust him, too, for each day's problems; live in vital union with him. *Colossians 2:6 (TLB)*

□ _____ □ _____

2. Let us therefore approach the throne of grace with fullest confidence, that we may receive mercy for our failures and grace to help in the hour of need. *Hebrews 4:16 (Phillips)* □ _____ □ _____

3. Let him have all your worries and cares, for he is always thinking about you and watching everything that concerns you. *1 Peter 5:7 (TLB)*

□ _____ □ _____

4. He did not even keep back his own Son, but offered him for us all! He gave us his Son—will he not also freely give us all things? *Romans 8:32 (TEV)*

□ _____ □ _____

5. Yet the Lord longs to be gracious to you; he rises to show you compassion. For the Lord is a God of justice. Blessed are all who wait for him! *Isaiah 30:18 (NIV)*

□ _____ □ _____

When I'm in a group I often fail to act like myself. Is it safe to be honest with God?

1. I will never turn away anyone who comes to me. *John 6:37 (TEV)* □_____ □_____

2. Lord, you have examined me and you know me. You know everything I do; from far away you understand all my thoughts. *Psalm 139:1-2 (TEV)*
□_____ □_____

3. He knows about everyone, everywhere. Everything about us is bare and wide open to the all-seeing eyes of our living God; nothing can be hidden from him to whom we must explain all that we have done. *Hebrews 4:13 (TLB)* □_____ □_____

4. GOD IS LIGHT and no shadow of darkness can exist in him. Consequently, if we were to say that we enjoyed fellowship with him and still went on living in darkness, we should be both telling and living a lie. But if we really are living in the same light in which he eternally exists, then we have true fellowship with each other, and the blood which his son Jesus shed for us keeps us clean from all sin. If we refuse to admit that we are sinners, then we live in a world of illusion and truth becomes a stranger to us. But if we freely admit that we have sinned, we find him reliable and just—he forgives our sins and makes us thoroughly clean from all that is evil. *1 John 1:5-9 (Phillips)* □_____ □_____

5. Sincerity and truth are what you require; fill my mind with your wisdom. *Psalm 51:6 (TEV)*
□_____ □_____

6. The sacrifices of God are a broken spirit; a broken and contrite heart, O God, you will not despise. *Psalm 51:17 (NIV)* □_____ □_____

34

Things are so impersonal at school. How can I be sure I'm not just a number to God?

1. Why, the very hairs of your heads are all numbered! Don't be afraid then; you are worth more than a great many sparrows! *Luke 12:7 (Phillips)*

☐_____ ☐_____

2. Yes, God has made an everlasting covenant with me; his agreement is eternal, final, sealed. He will constantly look after my safety and success. *2 Samuel 23:5 (TLB)*

☐_____ ☐_____

3. It is God himself who has set us apart, who placed his mark of ownership upon us, and who gave the Holy Spirit in our hearts as the guarantee of all that he has for us. *2 Corinthians 1:21–22 (TEV)*

☐_____ ☐_____

4. The sheep hear his voice as he calls his own sheep by name, and he leads them out. *John 10:3 (TEV)*

☐_____ ☐_____

5. Be glad because your names are written in heaven. *Luke 10:20 (TEV)*

☐_____ ☐_____

6. I am your God and will take care of you until you are old and your hair is gray. I made you and will care for you; I will give you help and rescue you. *Isaiah 46:4 (TEV)*

☐_____ ☐_____

Living with Myself

I'm even a stranger to myself these days. Does God know who I really am?

1. You created my inmost being; you knit me together in my mother's womb. I praise you because I am fearfully and wonderfully made; your works are wonderful, I know that full well. My frame was not hidden from you when I was made in the secret place. When I was woven together in the depths of the earth, your eyes saw my unformed body. *Psalm 139:13-15 (NIV)*
□ _____ □ _____

2. He has put his brand upon us—his mark of ownership—and given us his Holy Spirit in our hearts as guarantee that we belong to him, and as the first installment of all that he is going to give us. *2 Corinthians 1:22 (TLB)* □ _____ □ _____

3. All of us who are Christians . . . reflect like mirrors the glory of the Lord. We are transformed in ever-increasing splendour into his own image, and this is the work of the Lord who is the Spirit. *2 Corinthians 3:18 (Phillips)*
□ _____ □ _____

4. We who believe are carefully joined together with Christ as parts of a beautiful, constantly growing temple for God. And you also are joined with him and with each other by the Spirit, and are part of this dwelling place of God. *Ephesians 2:21-22 (TLB)*
□ _____ □ _____

5. You can buy two sparrows for a penny; yet not a single one of them falls to the ground without your Father's consent. As for you, even the hairs of your head have all been counted. So do not be afraid; you are worth much more than many sparrows! *Matthew 10:29-31 (TEV)* □ _____ □ _____

I don't know what to do with my life. Does God have dreams and plans for me?

1. I will instruct you and teach you in the way you should go; I will counsel you and watch over you. *Psalm 32:8 (NIV)* ☐_____ ☐_____

2. For I know the plans I have for you, declares the Lord, plans to prosper you and not to harm you, plans to give you hope and a future. *Jeremiah 29:11 (NIV)* ☐_____ ☐_____

3. I will teach you what you are to do. *Exodus 4:15 (NASB)* ☐_____ ☐_____

4. The Lord will fulfill his purpose for me; thy steadfast love, O Lord, endures for ever. *Psalm 138:8 (RSV)* ☐_____ ☐_____

5. You chart the path ahead of me, and tell me where to stop and rest. Every moment, you know where I am. You both precede and follow me, and place your hand of blessing on my head. *Psalm 139:3, 5 (TLB)* ☐_____ ☐_____

I feel like a walking disaster area. How can God still love me when I keep fouling things up?

1. As far as the east is from the west, so far has He removed our transgressions from us. Just as a father has compassion on his children, so the Lord has compassion on those who fear Him. For He Himself knows our frame; He is mindful that we are but dust. *Psalm 103:12-14 (NASB)* ☐_____ ☐_____

2. When I said, "My foot is slipping," your love, O Lord, supported me. *Psalm 94:18 (NIV)* ☐_____ ☐_____

3. But God demonstrates his own love for us in this: While we were still sinners, Christ died for us. *Romans 5:8 (NIV)* ☐_____ ☐_____

4. I will heal their waywardness and love them freely, for my anger has turned away from them. *Hosea 14:4 (NIV)* ☐_____ ☐_____

5. Let us never forget that our old selves died with him on the cross that the tyranny of sin over us might be broken—for a dead man can safely be said to be free from the power of sin. Look upon yourselves as dead to the appeal and power of sin but alive to God through Christ Jesus our Lord. *Romans 6:6-7, 11 (Phillips)* ☐_____ ☐_____

Everything I do is such a pale imitation of what I meant to do. Is God disappointed in me, too?

1. Commit everything you do to the Lord. Trust him to help you do it and he will. *Psalm 37:5 (TLB)* ☐_____ ☐_____

2. Fear not, for I am with you, be not dismayed, for I am your God; I will strengthen you, I will help you, I will uphold you with my victorious right hand. *Isaiah 41:10 (RSV)* ☐_____ ☐_____

3. He is patient with you, because he does not want anyone to be destroyed, but wants all to turn away from their sins. *2 Peter 3:9 (TEV)* ☐_____ ☐_____

4. In all these things we win an overwhelming victory through him who has proved his love for us. *Romans 8:37 (Phillips)* ☐_____ ☐_____

5. May the God who gives us peace make you holy in every way, and keep your whole being, spirit, soul, and body, free from all fault at the coming of our Lord Jesus Christ. He who calls you will do it, because he is faithful. *1 Thessalonians 5:23–24 (TEV)*

□_____ □_____

I feel as though life has given me a dirty rotten deal. Will God help me overcome my bitterness?

1. And God is able to make all grace abound to you, so that in all things at all times, having all that you need, you will abound in every good work. *2 Corinthians 9:8 (NIV)*

□_____ □_____

2. I have come in order that they might have life, life in all its fulness. *John 10:10 (TEV)*

□_____ □_____

3. Praise the Lord, my soul, and do not forget how kind he is. He forgives all my sins and heals all my diseases. He keeps me from the grave and blesses me with love and mercy. He fills my life with good things, so that I stay young and strong like an eagle. The Lord judges in favor of the oppressed and gives them their rights. *Psalm 103:2–6 (TEV)* □_____ □_____

4. Just as the sufferings of Christ flow over into our lives, so also through Christ our comfort overflows. *2 Corinthians 1:5 (NIV)* □_____ □_____

5. Let all bitterness, and wrath, and anger, and clamour, and evil speaking, be put away from you, with all malice: and be ye kind one to another, tenderhearted, forgiving one another, even as God for Christ's sake hath forgiven you. *Ephesians 4:31–32 (KJV)*

□_____ □_____

Nothing makes much sense to me any-more. How can I discover meaning in life?

1. Be rooted in him and founded upon him, continually strengthened by the faith as you were taught it and your lives will overflow with joy and thankfulness. *Colossians 2:7 (Phillips)* □ _____ □ _____

2. You love him, although you have not seen him. You believe in him, although you do not now see him. And so you rejoice with a great and glorious joy, which words cannot express, because you are receiving the purpose of your faith, the salvation of your souls. *1 Peter 1:8-9 (TEV)* □ _____ □ _____

3. For yourself, concentrate on winning God's approval, on being a workman with nothing to be ashamed of, and who knows how to use the word of truth to the best advantage. *2 Timothy 2:15 (Phillips)*
□ _____ □ _____

4. Let us give thanks to the God and Father of our Lord Jesus Christ! Because of his great mercy, he gave us new life by raising Jesus Christ from the dead. This fills us with a living hope, and so we look forward to possess the rich blessings that God keeps for his people. *2 Peter 1:3-4 (TEV)* □ _____ □ _____

5. For it is God who is at work within you, giving you the will and the power to achieve his purpose. *Philippians 2:13 (Phillips)* □ _____ □ _____

Sometimes I feel as though I simply can-not go on living. Where can I find reasons to keep hanging on?

1. Base your happiness on your hope in Christ. When trials come endure them patiently; steadfastly maintain the habit of prayer. *Romans 12:12 (Phillips)*

☐_____ ☐_____

2. May our Lord Jesus Christ himself and God our Father, who has loved us and given us everlasting comfort and hope which we don't deserve, comfort your hearts with all comfort, and help you in every good thing you say and do. *2 Thessalonians 2:16–17 (TLB)*

☐_____ ☐_____

3. For I am the Lord, your God, who takes hold of your right hand and says to you, Do not fear; I will help you. *Isaiah 41:13 (NIV)* ☐_____ ☐_____

4. If God is for us, who is against us? He who did not spare his own Son but gave him up for us all, will he not also give us all things with him? *Romans 8:31–32 (RSV)*

☐_____ ☐_____

5. It is he who saved us and chose us for his holy work, not because we deserved it but because that was his plan long before the world began—to show his love and kindness to us through Christ. *2 Timothy 1:9 (TLB)*

☐_____ ☐_____

6. Complete the salvation that God has given you with a proper sense of awe and responsibility. For it is God who is at work within you, giving you the will and the power to achieve his purpose. *Philippians 2:12–13 (Phillips)*

☐_____ ☐_____

I'm afraid I'm going to go crazy. Will God help me hold my pieces together?

1. To him who is able to keep you from falling and to present you before his glorious presence without fault and with great joy—to the only God our Savior be glory, majesty, power, and authority, through Jesus Christ our Lord, before all ages, now and forevermore! Amen. *Jude 1:24–25 (NIV)* ☐_____ ☐_____

2. I am with you; that is all you need. My power shows up best in weak people. Now I am glad to boast about how weak I am; I am glad to be a living demonstration of Christ's power, instead of showing off my own power and abilities. *2 Corinthians 12:9 (TLB)*
□_____ □_____

3. I have the strength to face all conditions by the power that Christ gives me. *Philippians 4:13 (TEV)*
□_____ □_____

4. The Lord himself will lead you and be with you. He will not fail you or abandon you, so do not lose courage or be afraid. *Deuteronomy 31:8 (TEV)*
□_____ □_____

5. Thou dost keep him in perfect peace, whose mind is stayed on thee, because he trusts in thee. *Isaiah 26:3 (RSV)* □_____ □_____

6. I am leaving you with a gift—peace of mind and heart! And the peace I give isn't fragile like the peace the world gives. So don't be troubled or afraid. *John 14:27 (TLB)*
□_____ □_____

Most days I feel as tense as a taut rubber band. Can I count on God to keep me from snapping apart?

1. Peace I leave with you; my own peace I give you. I do not give it to you as the world does. Do not be worried and upset; do not be afraid. *John 14:27 (TEV)*
□_____ □_____

2. Do not be anxious about anything, but in everything, by prayer and petition, with thanksgiving, present your requests to God. And the peace of God, which transcends all understanding, will guard your hearts and your minds in Christ Jesus. *Philippians 4:6-7 (NIV)*
□_____ □_____

3. The Lord gives strength to his people; the Lord blesses his people with peace. *Psalm 29:11 (NIV)*

□ _____ □ _____

4. God is our shelter and strength, always ready to help in times of trouble. *Psalm 46:1 (TEV)*

□ _____ □ _____

I feel so inferior to almost everyone. How do I rate in God's eyes?

1. He will hold you aloft in his hands for all to see—a splendid crown for the King of kings. Never again shall you be called "The God-forsaken Land" or the "Land that God Forgot." Your new name will be "The Land of God's Delight" and "The Bride," for the Lord delights in you and will claim you as his own. *Isaiah 62:3-4 (TLB)*

□ _____ □ _____

2. You are precious in my eyes, and honored, and I love you. *Isaiah 43:4 (RSV)*

□ _____ □ _____

3. God, what is man, that you should think of him; mere man, that you should care for him? You made him for a little while lower than the angels; you crowned him with glory and honor, and made him ruler over all things. *Hebrews 2:6-7 (TEV)*

□ _____ □ _____

I cry easily. Does God understand why?

1. You know how troubled I am; you have kept a record of my tears. Aren't they listed in your book? *Psalm 56:8 (TEV)* □ _____ □ _____

2. Praise be to the God and Father of our Lord Jesus Christ, the Father of compassion and the God of all comfort, who comforts us in all our troubles, so that we can comfort those in any trouble with the comfort we ourselves have received from God. *2 Corinthians 1:3-4 (NIV)* □_____ □_____

3. For the Lamb in the midst of the throne will be their shepherd, and he will guide them to springs of living water; and God will wipe away every tear from their eyes. *Revelation 7:17 (RSV)*
□_____ □_____

4. Those who sow in tears will reap with songs of joy. He who goes out weeping, carrying seed to sow, will return with songs of joy, carrying sheaves with him. *Psalm 126:5-6 (NIV)* □_____ □_____

5. He has sent me to comfort all who mourn, to give to those who mourn in Zion joy and gladness instead of grief, a song of praise instead of sorrow. *Isaiah 61:3 (TEV)* □_____ □_____

There are times when I get so angry I feel like throwing and smashing things. How does God want me to respond when I feel angry?

1. When the Holy Spirit controls our lives he will produce this kind of fruit in us: love, joy, peace, patience, kindness, goodness, faithfulness, gentleness and self-control. *Galatians 5:22 (TLB)*
□_____ □_____

2. If you are angry, don't sin by nursing your grudge. Don't let the sun go down with you still angry—get over it quickly; for when you are angry you give a mighty foothold to the devil. *Ephesians 4:26-27 (TLB)*
□_____ □_____

44

3. Be patient and wait for the Lord to act ... Don't give in to worry or anger; it only leads to trouble. *Psalm 37:7-8 (TEV)* □_____ □_____

4. Everyone should be quick to listen, slow to speak, and slow to become angry, for man's anger does not bring about the righteous life that God desires. *James 1:19-20 (TEV)* □_____ □_____

5. He who is slow to anger is better than the mighty, and he who rules his spirit, than he who captures a city. *Proverbs 16:32 (NASB)*
□_____ □_____

I get depressed every time I look in the mirror. How does God see me?

1. The Lord does not look at the things man looks at. Man looks at the outward appearance, but the Lord looks at the heart. *1 Samuel 16:7 (NIV)*
□_____ □_____

2. Worship the Lord with the beauty of holy lives. *Psalm 96:9 (TLB)* □_____ □_____

3. He has made everything beautiful in its time. *Ecclesiastes 3:11 (RSV)* □_____ □_____

4. The Lord their God will save them on that day as the flock of his people. They will sparkle in his land like jewels in a crown. How attractive and beautiful they will be! *Zechariah 9:16-17 (NIV)*
□_____ □_____

5. You should not use outward aids to make yourselves beautiful, such as the way you fix your hair, or the jewelry you put on, or the dresses you wear. Instead, your beauty should consist of your true inner self, the ageless beauty of a gentle and quiet spirit, which is of the greatest value in God's sight. *1 Peter 3:3-4 (TEV)*
□_____ □_____

I often feel panic when I think about the future. Where can I turn for help and reassurance?

1. Don't worry over anything whatever; whenever you pray tell God every detail of your needs in thankful prayer, and the peace of God, which surpasses human understanding, will keep constant guard over your hearts and minds as they rest in Christ Jesus. *Philippians 4:6–7 (Phillips)* □_____ □_____

2. I sought the Lord, and He answered me, and delivered me from all my fears. *Psalm 34:4 (NASB)*
□_____ □_____

3. Remember that I have commanded you to be determined and confident! Do not be afraid or discouraged, for I, the Lord your God, am with you wherever you go. *Joshua 1:9 (TEV)* □_____ □_____

4. The Lord watches over you—the Lord is your shade at your right hand; the sun will not harm you by day, nor the moon by night. The Lord will keep you from all harm—he will watch over your life; the Lord will watch over your coming and going both now and forevermore. *Psalm 121:5–8 (NIV)*
□_____ □_____

5. I will keep you strong and well. You will be like a garden that has plenty of water, like a spring of water that never goes dry. *Isaiah 58:11 (TEV)*
□_____ □_____

I get bored with life. Will God motivate and inspire me?

1. Delight yourselves in the Lord, yes, find your joy in him at all times . . . Never forget the nearness of your Lord. *Philippians 4:4–5 (Phillips)*
□_____ □_____

2. You will show me the path that leads to life; your presence fills me with joy and brings me pleasure forever. *Psalm 16:11 (TEV)*

☐＿＿＿＿＿＿ ☐＿＿＿＿＿＿

3. And whatever you do, whether in word or deed, do it all in the name of the Lord Jesus, giving thanks to God the Father through him. *Colossians 3:17 (NIV)*

☐＿＿＿＿＿＿ ☐＿＿＿＿＿＿

4. And let us not grow weary in well-doing, for in due season we shall reap, if we do not lose heart. *Galatians 6:9 (RSV)* ☐＿＿＿＿＿＿ ☐＿＿＿＿＿＿

Responsibility really scares me. Will God help me face up to what is expected of me?

1. I am ready for anything through the strength of the One who lives within me. *Philippians 4:13 (Phillips)*

☐＿＿＿＿＿＿ ☐＿＿＿＿＿＿

2. Do not fear, for I am with you; Do not anxiously look about you, for I am your God. I will strengthen you, surely I will help you, surely I will uphold you with My righteous right hand. *Isaiah 41:10 (NASB)*

☐＿＿＿＿＿＿ ☐＿＿＿＿＿＿

3. Trust in the Lord with all your heart, and do not rely on your own insight. In all your ways acknowledge him, and he will make straight your paths. *Proverbs 3:5–6 (RSV)* ☐＿＿＿＿＿＿ ☐＿＿＿＿＿＿

4. This faith of ours is the only way in which the world can be conquered. For who could ever be said to conquer the world but the man who really believes that Jesus is God's Son? *1 John 5:4–5 (Phillips)*

☐＿＿＿＿＿＿ ☐＿＿＿＿＿＿

I feel tired all the time. Can God give me the energy I need?

1. He strengthens those who are weak and tired. *Isaiah 40:29 (TEV)* □ _____ □ _____

2. But those who hope in the Lord will renew their strength. They will soar on wings like eagles; they will run and not grow weary, they will walk and not be faint. *Isaiah 40:31 (NIV)* □ _____ □ _____

3. The Sovereign Lord is my strength; he makes my feet like the feet of a deer, he enables me to go on the heights. *Habakkuk 3:19 (NIV)*
□ _____ □ _____

4. Trust in the Lord God always, for in the Lord Jehovah is your everlasting strength. *Isaiah 26:4 (TLB)*
□ _____ □ _____

5. Let the beloved of the Lord rest secure in him, for he shields him all day long, and the one the Lord loves rests between his shoulders. *Deuteronomy 33:12 (NIV)*
□ _____ □ _____

I often feel the need to get high on drugs. Can I depend on God instead of drugs to fulfill and free me?

1. To have your mind controlled by human nature results in death; to have your mind controlled by the Spirit results in life and peace. *Romans 8:6 (TEV)*
□ _____ □ _____

2. For the Lord to whom they could turn is the Spirit, and wherever the Spirit of the Lord is, men's souls are set free. *2 Corinthians 3:17 (Phillips)*
□ _____ □ _____

3. If the Son makes you free, then you will be really free. *John 8:36 (TEV)* □ _____ □ _____

4. He who did not grudge his own Son but gave him up for us all—can we not trust such a God to give us, with him, everything else that we can need? *Romans 8:32 (Phillips)* □_____ □_____

5. My God will supply all that you need from his glorious resources in Christ Jesus. *Philippians 4:19 (Phillips)* □_____ □_____

Sometimes I drink too much and I seem to flunk every diet I try. How can I let God control my life instead of my being controlled by food and alcohol?

1. Because he himself suffered when he was tempted, he is able to help those who are being tempted. *Hebrews 2:18 (NIV)* □_____ □_____

2. Learn to put aside your own desires so that you will become patient and godly, gladly letting God have his way with you. *2 Peter 1:6 (TLB)* □_____ □_____

3. The Lord knows how to rescue godly men from their trials. *2 Peter 2:9 (TEV)* □_____ □_____

4. Blessed is the man who endures trial, for when he has stood the test he will receive the crown of life which God has promised to those who love him. Let no one say when he is tempted, "I am tempted by God"; for God cannot be tempted with evil and he himself tempts no one; but each person is tempted when he is lured and enticed by his own desire. *James 1:12–14 (RSV)* □_____ □_____

5. Don't be vague but grasp firmly what you know to be the will of the Lord. Don't get stimulus from wine (for there is always the danger of excessive drinking), but let the Spirit stimulate your souls. *Ephesians 5:17–18 (Phillips)* □_____ □_____

6. Do not be anxious about your life, what you shall eat, nor about your body, what you shall put on. For life is more than food, and the body more than clothing. *Luke 12:22–23 (RSV)* □_____ □_____

7. In all these things we are more than conquerors through him that loved us. *Romans 8:37 (KJV)*
□_____ □_____

I feel so guilty because of my problems with masturbation and lust. Can God help me overcome these temptations?

1. Every temptation that has come your way is the kind that normally comes to people. But God keeps his promise, and he will not allow you to be tempted beyond your power to resist; at the time you are tempted he will give you the strength to endure it, and so provide you with a way out. *1 Corinthians 10:13 (TEV)*
□_____ □_____

2. How can a young man keep his way pure? By living according to your word. I seek you with all my heart; do not let me stray from your commands. *Psalm 119:9–10 (NIV)* □_____ □_____

3. You are God's man. Run from all these evil things and work instead at what is right and good, learning to trust him and love others, and to be patient and gentle. *1 Timothy 6:11 (TLB)*
□_____ □_____

4. But the Lord is faithful. He will make you strong and keep you safe from the Evil One. *2 Thessalonians 3:3 (TEV)* □_____ □_____

5. Submit therefore to God. Resist the devil and he will flee from you. Draw near to God and he will draw near to you. *James 4:7–8 (NASB)*
□_____ □_____

6. Let the Spirit direct your lives, and do not satisfy the desires of the human nature. For what our human nature wants is opposed to what the Spirit wants, and what the Spirit wants is opposed to what human nature wants. The two are enemies, and this means that you cannot do what you want to do. And those who belong to Christ Jesus have put to death their human nature, with all its passions and desires. The Spirit has given us life; he must also control our lives. *Galatians 5:16–17, 24–25 (TEV)*
□ _____ □ _____

I've had sexual intercourse and now I suffer tremendous guilt. Will God forgive me and help me to go on?

1. But if we confess our sins to God, he will keep his promise and do what is right: he will forgive us our sins and make us clean from all our wrongdoing. *1 John 1:9 (TEV)* □ _____ □ _____

2. You have been cleansed from sin; you have been dedicated to God; you have been put right with God through the name of the Lord Jesus Christ and by the Spirit of our God. *1 Corinthians 6:11 (TEV)*
□ _____ □ _____

3. In this man Jesus, there is forgiveness for your sins! Everyone who trusts in him is freed from all guilt and declared righteous. *Acts 13:38–39 (TLB)*
□ _____ □ _____

4. For if a man is in Christ he becomes a new person altogether—the past is finished and gone, everything has become fresh and new. *2 Corinthians 5:17 (Phillips)*
□ _____ □ _____

5. He does not punish us as we deserve or repay us for our sins and wrongs. As far as the east is from the west, so far does he remove our sins from us. *Psalm 103:10, 12 (TEV)* □ _____ □ _____

6. He will again have compassion upon us, he will tread our iniquities under foot. Thou wilt cast all our sins into the depths of the sea. *Micah 7:19 (RSV)*
☐_____ ☐_____

I feel sick much of the time. Will God help me back to health?

1. But I will restore you to health and heal your wounds, declares the Lord. *Jeremiah 30:17 (NIV)*
☐_____ ☐_____

2. I am the Lord who heals you. *Exodus 15:26 (NIV)*
☐_____ ☐_____

3. Jesus . . . healed all who were sick. He did this to make come true what the prophet Isaiah had said, "He himself took our illnesses and carried away our diseases." *Matthew 8:16-17 (TEV)*
☐_____ ☐_____

4. And I will always guide you and satisfy you with good things. I will keep you strong and well. You will be like a garden that has plenty of water, like a spring of water that never runs dry. *Isaiah 58:11 (TEV)*
☐_____ ☐_____

5. But for you who obey me, my saving power will rise on you like the sun and bring healing like the sun's rays. *Malachi 4:2 (TEV)* ☐_____ ☐_____

What is happening in the world is very frightening. How can I know God is still in control?

1. The Lord will settle international disputes; all the nations will convert their weapons of war into implements of peace. Then at the last all wars will stop and all military training will end. *Isaiah 2:4 (TLB)*

□_____ □_____

2. Everyone here will see that the Lord does not need swords or spears to save his people. He is victorious in battle, and he will put all of you in our power. 1 Samuel 17:47 (TEV) □_____ □_____

3. Those who trust in the Lord are like Mount Zion, which cannot be shaken but endures forever. As the mountains surround Jerusalem, so the Lord surrounds his people both now and forevermore. *Psalm 125:1-2 (NIV)* □_____ □_____

4. Let him have all your worries and cares, for he is always thinking about you and watching everything that concerns you. *1 Peter 5:7 (TLB)*

□_____ □_____

5. Do not be afraid of your enemies or lose courage or panic. The Lord your God is going with you, and he will give you victory. *Deuteronomy 20:3-4 (TEV)*

□_____ □_____

I'm afraid of dying. Will God take care of me?

1. He will swallow up death for ever, and the Lord God will wipe away tears from all faces, and the reproach of his people he will take away from all the earth, for the Lord has spoken. *Isaiah 25:8 (RSV)*

□_____ □_____

2. I give them eternal life, and they shall never perish; no one can snatch them out of my hand. *John 10:28 (NIV)*

□_____ □_____

3. The world and its desires pass away, but the man who does the will of God lives forever. *1 John 2:17 (NIV)*

□_____ □_____

53

4. Even though I walk through the valley of the shadow of death, I fear no evil; for thou art with me; thy rod and thy staff, they comfort me. *Psalm 23:4 (RSV)*
□ _____ □ _____

5. If the Spirit of God, who raised Jesus from death, lives in you, then he who raised Christ from death will also give life to your mortal bodies by the presence of his Spirit in you. *Romans 8:11 (TEV)*
□ _____ □ _____

6. Since the children have flesh and blood, he too shared in their humanity so that by his death he might destroy him who holds the power of death—that is, the devil—and free those who all their lives were held in slavery by their fear of death. *Hebrews 2:14-15 (NIV)*
□ _____ □ _____

I have horrible nightmares when I sleep. Can God transform my night terrors into restful sleep?

1. When you lie down, you will not be afraid; when you lie down, your sleep will be sweet. *Proverbs 3:24 (NASB)*
□ _____ □ _____

2. He will cover you with his wings; you will be safe in his care; his faithfulness will protect and defend you. You need not fear any dangers at night or sudden attacks during the day or the plagues that strike in the dark or the evils that kill in daylight. *Psalm 91:4-5 (TEV)*
□ _____ □ _____

3. I will lie down and sleep in peace, for you alone, O Lord, make me dwell in safety. *Psalm 4:8 (NIV)*
□ _____ □ _____

4. And the Lord gave them rest on every side. *Joshua 21:44 (NASB)* □ _____ □ _____

Worrying often keeps me awake at night. Does God have anything to offer an insomniac like me?

1. Peace I leave with you; my peace I give you. I do not give to you as the world gives. Do not let your hearts be troubled and do not be afraid. *John 14:27 (NIV)*

☐＿＿＿＿＿＿ ☐＿＿＿＿＿＿

2. There still exists a full and complete rest for the people of God. *Hebrews 4:9 (Phillips)*

☐＿＿＿＿＿＿ ☐＿＿＿＿＿＿

3. I lie down and sleep, and all night long the Lord protects me. *Psalm 3:5 (TEV)*

☐＿＿＿＿＿＿ ☐＿＿＿＿＿＿

4. In vain you rise early and stay up late, toiling for food to eat—for he grants sleep to those he loves. *Psalm 127:2 (NIV)* ☐＿＿＿＿＿＿ ☐＿＿＿＿＿＿

I have a big mouth. How can I develop more discretion in what I say?

1. Set a guard, O Lord, over my mouth; keep watch over the door of my lips. *Psalm 141:3 (NASB)*

☐＿＿＿＿＿＿ ☐＿＿＿＿＿＿

2. He who guards his mouth and his tongue, guards his soul from troubles. *Proverbs 21:23 (NASB)*

☐＿＿＿＿＿＿ ☐＿＿＿＿＿＿

3. The more you talk, the more likely you are to sin. If you are wise, you will keep quiet. *Proverbs 10:19 (TEV)*

☐＿＿＿＿＿＿ ☐＿＿＿＿＿＿

4. Do not use harmful words in talking. Use only helpful words, the kind that build up and provide what is needed, so that what you say will do good to those who hear you. Nor is it fitting for you to use obscene, foolish, or dirty words. Rather you should give thanks to God. *Ephesians 4:29, 5:4 (TEV)* ☐＿＿＿＿＿＿ ☐＿＿＿＿＿＿

5. Reckless words pierce like a sword, but the tongue of the wise brings healing. *Proverbs 12:18 (NIV)*
☐＿＿＿＿＿＿ ☐＿＿＿＿＿＿

6. If anyone considers himself religious and yet does not keep a tight rein on his tongue, he deceives himself and his religion is worthless. *James 1:26 (NIV)*
☐＿＿＿＿＿＿ ☐＿＿＿＿＿＿

Jobs are hard to find and there's not enough money to pay the bills. Will God take care of me?

1. My God, with all his abundant wealth in Christ Jesus, will supply all your needs. *Philippians 4:19 (TEV)*
☐＿＿＿＿＿＿ ☐＿＿＿＿＿＿

2. God is able to give you more than you need, so that you will always have all you need for yourselves and more than enough for every good cause. *2 Corinthians 9:8 (TEV)* ☐＿＿＿＿＿＿ ☐＿＿＿＿＿＿

3. The lions may grow weak and hungry, but those who seek the Lord lack no good thing. *Psalm 34:10 (NIV)*
☐＿＿＿＿＿＿ ☐＿＿＿＿＿＿

4. I have never seen a good man abandoned by the Lord or his children begging for food. *Psalm 37:25 (TEV)*
☐＿＿＿＿＿＿ ☐＿＿＿＿＿＿

5. He who did not grudge his own Son but gave him up for us all—can we not trust such a God to give us, with him, everything else that we can need? *Romans 8:32 (Phillips)* ☐＿＿＿＿＿＿ ☐＿＿＿＿＿＿

6. The Lord is my shepherd, I shall lack nothing. *Psalm 23:1 (NIV)* ☐＿＿＿＿＿＿ ☐＿＿＿＿＿＿

The important people in my life often have abandoned me. Now I don't trust anyone. How do I know God won't desert me, too?

1. For God has said, "I will never leave you; I will never abandon you." *Hebrews 13:5 (TEV)*
☐＿＿＿＿＿ ☐＿＿＿＿＿

2. Remember, I am with you always, even to the end of the world. *Matthew 28:20 (Phillips)*
☐＿＿＿＿＿ ☐＿＿＿＿＿

3. For the Lord your God is a merciful God; he will not abandon or destroy you or forget the covenant with your forefathers, which he confirmed to them by oath. *Deuteronomy 4:31 (NIV)*
☐＿＿＿＿＿ ☐＿＿＿＿＿

4. The Lord loves what is right and does not abandon his faithful people. He protects them forever. *Psalm 37:28 (TEV)* ☐＿＿＿＿＿ ☐＿＿＿＿＿

5. The mountains and hills may crumble, but my love for you will never end; I will keep forever my promise of peace. So says the Lord who loves you. *Isaiah 54:10 (TEV)* ☐＿＿＿＿＿ ☐＿＿＿＿＿

I feel as though no one really knows me. How deeply does God know and understand me?

1. O Lord, you have searched me and you know me. You know when I sit and when I rise; you perceive my thoughts from afar. You discern my going out and my lying down; you are familiar with all my ways. *Psalm 139:1-3 (NIV)* ☐＿＿＿＿＿ ☐＿＿＿＿＿

2. Your knowledge of me is too deep; it is beyond my understanding. *Psalm 139:6 (TEV)*

☐_____ ☐_____

3. You made all the delicate, inner parts of my body, and knit them together in my mother's womb. You were there while I was being formed in utter seclusion! You saw me before I was born and scheduled each day of my life before I began to breathe. *Psalm 139:13, 15–16 (TLB)*

☐_____ ☐_____

4. When my spirit grows faint within me, it is you who know my way. *Psalm 142:3 (NIV)*

☐_____ ☐_____

5. But you are our father, Lord. We are like clay, and you are like the potter. You created us. *Isaiah 64:8 (TEV)* ☐_____ ☐_____

I feel as if I don't belong anywhere. Where do I fit in God's plans?

1. It is God himself who has made us what we are and given us new lives from Christ Jesus; and long ages ago he planned that we should spend these lives in helping others. *Ephesians 2:10 (TLB)*

☐_____ ☐_____

2. If anyone is in Christ, he is a new creation; the old has gone, the new has come! All this is from God, who reconciled us to himself through Christ and gave us the ministry of reconciliation: that God was reconciling the world to himself in Christ, not counting men's sins against them. And he has committed to us the message of reconciliation. We are therefore Christ's ambassadors, as though God were making his appeal through us. *2 Corinthians 5:17–20 (NIV)*

☐_____ ☐_____

50

3. You may live a life worthy of the Lord and may please him in every way: bearing fruit in every good work, growing in the knowledge of God, being strengthened with all power according to his glorious might so that you may have great endurance and patience, and joyfully giving thanks to the Father, who has qualified you to share in the inheritance of the saints in the kingdom of light. *Colossians 1:10–12 (NIV)*

☐_____ ☐_____

4. Go into all the world and preach the good news to all creation. *Mark 16:15 (NIV)*

☐_____ ☐_____

5. Do you not know that you are God's temple and that God's Spirit dwells in you? *1 Corinthians 3:16 (RSV)*

☐_____ ☐_____

Living with My Family and Others

My parents are always fighting. I'm afraid they are going to get a divorce. What do I have to hold on to?

1. Whoever goes to the Lord for safety, whoever remains under the protection of the Almighty, can say to him, "You are my defender and protector. You are my God; in you I trust." He will cover you with his wings; you will be safe in his care; his faithfulness will protect and defend you. *Psalm 91:1-2, 4 (TEV)*

□_____ □_____

2. Because he loves me, says the Lord, I will rescue him; I will protect him, for he acknowledges my name. He will call upon me, and I will answer him; I will be with him in trouble, I will deliver him and honor him. *Psalm 91:14-15 (NIV)* □_____ □_____

3. Surely God is my help; the Lord is the one who sustains me. *Psalm 54:4 (NIV)*

□_____ □_____

4. I sought the Lord, and he answered me, and delivered me from all my fears. *Psalm 34:4 (RSV)*

□_____ □_____

My parents simply don't understand me. Can God help us to communicate?

1. Children, obey your parents in the Lord, for this is right. "Honor your father and mother"—which is the first commandment with a promise—"that it may go well with you and that you may enjoy long life on the earth." *Ephesians 6:1-3 (NIV)*

□_____ □_____

2. You are the people of God; he loved you and chose you for his own. So then, you must put on compassion, kindness, humility, gentleness, and patience. Be helpful to one another, and forgive one another, whenever any of you has a complaint against someone else. You must forgive each other in the same way that the Lord has forgiven you. And to all these add love, which binds all things together in perfect unity. *Colossians 3:12-14 (TEV)* □_____ □_____

3. Everyone should be quick to listen, slow to speak, and slow to become angry. *James 1:19 (NIV)*
□_____ □_____

4. Listen to your father; without him you would not exist. When your mother is old, show her your appreciation. *Proverbs 23:22 (TEV)*
□_____ □_____

My parents are divorced and I'm caught in the middle. Can God help me deal with this situation without being torn apart?

1. The eternal God is your dwelling place, and underneath are the everlasting arms. *Deuteronomy 33:27 (RSV)* □_____ □_____

2. Let the beloved of the Lord rest secure in him, for he shields him all day long, and the one the Lord loves rests between his shoulders. *Deuteronomy 33:12 (NIV)*
□_____ □_____

3. For I, the Lord your God, hold your right hand; it is I who say to you, "Fear not, I will help you." *Isaiah 41:13 (RSV)* □_____ □_____

4. My father and mother may abandon me, but the Lord will take care of me. *Psalm 27:10 (TEV)*
□_____ □_____

5. My soul finds rest in God alone; my salvation comes from him. He alone is my rock and my salvation; he is my fortress, I will never be shaken. *Psalm 62:1–2 (NIV)*

☐ _____ ☐ _____

My father rarely was around while I was growing up, so I've never really known what it's like to have a father. Will God be a father to me?

1. I will be a father to you, and you will be my sons and daughters, says the Lord Almighty. *2 Corinthians 6:18 (NIV)* ☐ _____ ☐ _____

2. To show that you are his sons, God sent the Spirit of his Son into our hearts, the Spirit who cries, "Father, my Father." *Galatians 4:6 (TEV)*

☐ _____ ☐ _____

3. He is like a father to us, tender and sympathetic to those who reverence him. *Psalm 103:13 (TLB)*

☐ _____ ☐ _____

4. You are my father and my God; you are my protector and savior. *Psalm 89:26 (TEV)*

☐ _____ ☐ _____

5. Consider the incredible love that the Father has shown us in allowing us to be called "children of God"— and that is not just what we are called, but what we *are*. *1 John 3:1 (Phillips)*

☐ _____ ☐ _____

My mother is terminally ill. How can God help us to cope?

1. The Lord is close to the brokenhearted and saves those who are crushed in spirit. *Psalm 34:18 (NIV)*

☐ _____ ☐ _____

2. Blessed be the God and Father of our Lord Jesus Christ, the Father of mercies and God of all comfort, who comforts us in all our affliction, so that we may be able to comfort those who are in any affliction, with the comfort with which we ourselves are comforted by God. For as we share abundantly in Christ's sufferings, so through Christ we share abundantly in comfort too. *2 Corinthians 1:3-5 (RSV)*

☐_____ ☐_____

3. We can rejoice, too, when we run into problems and trials for we know that they are good for us—they help us learn to be patient. And patience develops strength of character in us and helps us trust God more each time we use it until finally our hope and faith are strong and steady. Then, when that happens, we are able to hold our heads high no matter what happens and know that all is well, for we know how dearly God loves us, and we feel this warm love everywhere within us because God has given us the Holy Spirit to fill our hearts with his love. *Romans 5:3-5 (TLB)*

☐_____ ☐_____

4. Base your happiness on your hope in Christ. When trials come endure them patiently; steadfastly maintain the habit of prayer. *Romans 12:12 (Phillips)*

☐_____ ☐_____

5. We know that to those who love God, who are called according to his plan, everything that happens fits into a pattern for good. *Romans 8:28 (Phillips)*

☐_____ ☐_____

Someone I really loved has just been killed in a car accident. Will God help me out of my depression?

1. I, even I, am he who comforts you. *Isaiah 51:12 (NIV)*

☐_____ ☐_____

2. As a mother comforts her child, so will I comfort you. *Isaiah 66:13 (NIV)* □ _____ □ _____

3. God himself shall be with them, and will wipe away every tear from their eyes. Death shall be no more, and never again shall there be sorrow or crying or pain. For all those former things are past and gone. *Revelation 21:3-4 (Phillips)* □ _____ □ _____

4. Where, Death, is your victory? Where, Death, is your power to hurt? But thanks be to God who gives us the victory through our Lord Jesus Christ! *1 Corinthians 15:55, 57 (TEV)* □ _____ □ _____

5. He heals the brokenhearted, and binds up their wounds. *Psalm 147:3 (RSV)*
□ _____ □ _____

My parents, boss and teachers nag me continually. How does God want me to respond to authorities in my life?

1. Submit to one another out of reverence for Christ. *Ephesians 5:21 (NIV)*
□ _____ □ _____

2. Everyone must submit himself to the governing authorities, for there is no authority except that which God has established. The authorities that exist have been established by God. *Romans 13:1 (NIV)*
□ _____ □ _____

3. Slaves, obey your masters in everything; and do it, not only when their eye is on you and to win their favor, but with sincerity of heart and reverence for the Lord. Whatever you do, work at it with all your heart, as working for the Lord, not for men, since you know that you will receive an inheritance from the Lord as a reward. It is the Lord Christ you are serving. *Colossians 3:22-24 (NIV)* □ _____ □ _____

4. Obey your leaders and submit to their authority. They keep watch over you as men who must give an account. Obey them so that their work will be a joy, not a burden, for that would be of no advantage to you. *Hebrews 13:17 (NIV)* □_____ □_____

My family isn't Christian and they ridicule my faith and laugh when I talk about God. How should I relate to them?

1. It is God's will that your good lives should silence those who foolishly condemn the Gospel without knowing what it can do for them, having never experienced its power. You are free from the law, but that doesn't mean you are free to do wrong. Live as those who are free to do only God's will at all times. Show respect for everyone. *1 Peter 2:15–17 (TLB)*
□_____ □_____

2. The Lord's servant must not quarrel. He must be kind toward all, a good and patient teacher, who is gentle as he corrects his opponents, for it may be that God will give them the opportunity to repent and come to know the truth. *2 Timothy 2:24–25 (TEV)*
□_____ □_____

3. Your life must be controlled by love, just as Christ loved us and gave his life for us as a sweet-smelling offering and sacrifice that pleases God. *Ephesians 5:2 (TEV)* □_____ □_____

4. And whatever you do or say, let it be as a representative of the Lord Jesus, and come with him into the presence of God the Father to give him your thanks. *Colossians 3:17 (TLB)*
□_____ □_____

My desire to follow Jesus causes friction and division between me and my skeptical family. Is this really God's will?

1. Don't imagine that I came to bring peace to the earth! No, rather, a sword. I have come to set a man against his father, and a daughter against her mother, and a daughter-in-law against her mother-in-law—a man's worst enemies will be right in his own home! If you love your father and mother more than you love me, you are not worthy of being mine; or if you love your son or daughter more than me, you are not worthy of being mine. *Matthew 10:34-37 (TLB)*
☐_____ ☐_____

2. "I tell you the truth," Jesus replied, "no one who has left home or brothers or sisters or mother or father or children or fields for me and the gospel will fail to receive a hundred times as much in this present age (homes, brothers, sisters, mothers, children and fields—and with them, persecutions) and in the age to come, eternal life." *Mark 10:29-30 (NIV)*
☐_____ ☐_____

3. Though my father and mother forsake me, the Lord will receive me. Teach me your way, O Lord; lead me in a straight path because of my oppressors. *Psalm 27:10-11 (NIV)* ☐_____ ☐_____

I'm adopted and my parents treat me differently from their natural children. Will God consider me as one of his true children?

1. So you are no longer outsiders or aliens, but fellow-citizens with every other Christian—you belong now to the household of God. *Ephesians 2:19 (Phillips)*
☐_____ ☐_____

2. The Spirit himself endorses our inward conviction that we really are the children of God. Think what that means. If we are his children then we are God's heirs, and all that Christ inherits will belong to all of us as well! Yes, if we share in his sufferings we shall certainly share in his glory. *Romans 8:16–17 (Phillips)*

☐_____ ☐_____

3. Yet to all who received him, to those who believed in his name, he gave the right to become children of God. *John 1:12 (NIV)* ☐_____ ☐_____

I'm so lonely and homesick I feel as if I'm going to die. Does God understand how I feel?

1. I will not leave you as orphans; I will come to you. *John 14:18 (NIV)* ☐_____ ☐_____

2. He gives the lonely a home to live in and leads prisoners out into happy freedom. *Psalms 68:6 (TEV)*

☐_____ ☐_____

3. Then you shall call, and the Lord will answer; you shall cry, and he will say, Here I am. *Isaiah 58:9 (RSV)*

☐_____ ☐_____

4. So you have everything when you have Christ, and you are filled with God through your union with Christ. *Colossians 2:10 (TLB)*

☐_____ ☐_____

I often argue and disagree with my brothers and sisters. Can God help my relationships with them?

1. Help your brother and he will protect you like a strong city wall, but if you quarrel with him, he will close

his doors to you. *Proverbs 18:19 (TEV)*
□_____ □_____

2. If anyone says "I love God," but keeps on hating his brother, he is a liar; for if he doesn't love his brother who is right there in front of him, how can he love God whom he has never seen? And God himself has said that one must love not only God, but his brother too. *1 John 4:20–21 (TLB)* □_____ □_____

3. A true friend is always loyal, and a brother is born to help in time of need. *Proverbs 17:17 (TLB)*
□_____ □_____

4. If your brother sins against you, go to him and show him his fault. But do it privately, just between yourselves. If he listens to you, you have won your brother back. *Matthew 18:15 (TEV)*
□_____ □_____

All my friends are getting married. Will God guide me to a mate who is right for me?

1. I alone know the plans I have for you, plans to bring you prosperity and not disaster, plans to bring about the future you hope for. *Jeremiah 29:11 (TEV)*
□_____ □_____

2. Remember the Lord in everything you do, and he will show you the right way. *Proverbs 3:6 (TEV)*
□_____ □_____

3. You open your hand and satisfy the desires of every living thing. The Lord is righteous in all his ways and loving toward all he has made. The Lord is near to all who call on him, to all who call on him in truth. He fulfills the desires of those who fear him; he hears their cry and saves them. *Psalm 145:16–19 (NIV)*
□_____ □_____

4. You chart the path ahead of me, and tell me where to

stop and rest. Every moment, you know where I am. You both precede and follow me, and place your hand of blessing on my head. *Psalm 139:3, 5 (TLB)*

5. The Lord will fulfill his purpose for me; your love, O Lord, endures forever. *Psalm 138:8 (NIV)*

☐ _____ ☐ _____

I get scared when I think about spending the rest of my life with someone in a marriage relationship. Can God help me love someone that long?

1. As, therefore, God's picked representatives, purified and beloved, put on that nature which is merciful in action, kindly in heart, and humble in mind. Accept life, and be most patient and tolerant with one another, always ready to forgive if you have a difference with anyone. Forgive as freely as the Lord has forgiven you. And above everything else, be truly loving, for love binds all the virtues together in perfection. *Colossians 3:12–14 (Phillips)* ☐ _____ ☐ _____

2. Wives, adapt yourselves to your husbands; that is your Christian duty. Husbands, give your wives much love; never treat them harshly. *Colossians 3:18–19 (Phillips)* ☐ _____ ☐ _____

3. Let every one of you who is a husband love his wife as he loves himself, and let every wife respect her husband. *Ephesians 5:33 (Phillips)*

☐ _____ ☐ _____

4. Haven't you read that at the beginning the Creator "made them male and female," and said, "For this reason a man will leave his father and mother and be united to his wife, and the two will become one flesh"? So they are no longer two, but one. Therefore what God has joined together, let man not separate. *Matthew 19:4–6 (NIV)* ☐ _____ ☐ _____

There's so much pressure to go along with the crowd. Will God help me to be strong for him?

1. Whatever you do or say, let it be as a representative of the Lord Jesus, and come with him into the presence of God the Father to give him your thanks. *Colossians 3:17 (TLB)* □_____ □_____

2. Do everything without complaining or arguing, so that you may become blameless and pure, children of God without fault in a crooked and depraved generation, in which you shine like stars in the universe as you hold out the word of life. *Philippians 2:14–16 (NIV)*
□_____ □_____

3. Quietly trust yourself to Christ your Lord and if anybody asks why you believe as you do, be ready to tell him, and do it in a gentle and respectful way. Do what is right; then if men speak against you, calling you evil names, they will become ashamed of themselves for falsely accusing you when you have only done what is good. *1 Peter 3:15–16 (TLB)*
□_____ □_____

There are a lot of cliques in school and I never seem to fit in. Does God understand my feelings of rejection?

1. If the world hates you, you know that it hated me first. If you belonged to the world, the world would love its own. But because you do not belong to the world and I have chosen you out of it, the world will hate you. *John 15:18–19 (Phillips)* □_____ □_____

2. We despised him and rejected him; he endured suffering and pain. No one would even look at him—we ignored him as if he were nothing. But he endured the suffering that should have been ours, the pain that we should have borne. We are healed by the punishment he suffered, made whole by the blows he received. *Isaiah 53:3-5 (TEV)* □ _____ □ _____

3. Blessed are you when people insult you, persecute you and falsely say all kinds of evil against you because of me. Rejoice and be glad, because great is your reward in heaven, for in the same way they persecuted the prophets who were before you. *Matthew 5:11-12 (NIV)*

□ _____ □ _____

4. Even though you are so high above, you care for the lowly . . . When I am surrounded by troubles, you keep me safe. You oppose my angry enemies and save me by your power. *Psalm 138:6-7 (TEV)*

□ _____ □ _____

My interests are often different from those of others in my age group. What does God want me to care about?

1. You have been raised to life with Christ. Set your hearts, then, on the things that are in heaven, where Christ sits on his throne at the right side of God. Keep your minds fixed on things there, not on things here on earth. *Colossians 3:1-2 (TEV)*

□ _____ □ _____

2. Fill your minds with those things that are good and deserve praise: things that are true, noble, right, pure, lovely, and honorable. Put into practice what you learned and received from me, both from my words and from my deeds. And the God who gives us peace will be with you. *Philippians 4:8-9 (TEV)*

□ _____ □ _____

3. Be imitators of God, therefore, as dearly loved children and live a life of love, just as Christ loved us and

gave himself up for us as a fragrant offering and sacrifice
to God. *Ephesians 5:1–2 (NIV)*

□_____ □_____

4. Through Jesus, therefore, let us continually offer to
God a sacrifice of praise—the fruit of lips that confess his
name. And do not forget to do good and to share with
others, for with such sacrifices God is pleased. *Hebrews
13:15–16 (NIV)* □_____ □_____

All the "weirdos" seem to be attracted to me. Can God help me to love all my brothers and sisters?

1. For though we have never yet seen God, when we
love each other God lives in us and his love within us
grows ever stronger. *1 John 4:12 (TLB)*

□_____ □_____

2. You should be like one big happy family, full of sym-
pathy toward each other, loving one another with tender
hearts and humble minds. Don't repay evil for evil. Don't
snap back at those who say unkind things about you.
Instead, pray for God's help for them, for we are to be
kind to others, and God will bless us for it. *1 Peter 3:8–9
(TLB)* □_____ □_____

3. This is how we know what love is: Jesus Christ laid
down his life for us. And we ought to lay down our lives
for our brothers. *1 John 3:16 (NIV)*

□_____ □_____

4. I pray that your love will keep on growing more and
more, together with true knowledge and perfect judg-
ment, so that you will be able to choose what is best.
Then you will be free from all impurity and blame on the
Day of Christ. *Philippians 1:9–10 (TEV)*

□_____ □_____

My roommate is driving me nuts. How does God put up with such an obnoxious individual?

1. But God has shown us how much he loves us; it was while we were still sinners that Christ died for us! *Romans 5:8 (TEV)* □_____ □_____

2. And I pray that Christ will be more and more at home in your hearts, living within you as you trust in him. May your roots go down deep into the soil of God's marvelous love; and may you be able to feel and understand, as all God's children should, how long, how wide, how deep, and how high his love really is; and to experience this love for yourselves, though it is so great that you will never see the end of it or fully know or understand it. And so at last you will be filled up with God himself. *Ephesians 3:17–19 (TLB)*

□_____ □_____

3. Love is patient and kind; love is not jealous or boastful; it is not arrogant or rude. Love does not insist on its own way; it is not irritable or resentful; it does not rejoice at wrong, but rejoices in the right. Love bears all things, believes all things, hopes all things, endures all things. *1 Corinthians 13:4–7 (RSV)*

□_____ □_____

I feel like getting even when someone has insulted me. Can God help me get rid of such feelings?

1. Do not repay evil with evil or insult with insult, but with blessing, because to this you were called so that you may inherit a blessing. *1 Peter 3:9 (NIV)*

□_____ □_____

2. Rest in the Lord; wait patiently for him to act. Don't be envious of evil men who prosper. Stop your anger!

Turn off your wrath. Don't fret and worry—it only leads to harm. For the wicked shall be destroyed, but those who trust the Lord shall be given every blessing. *Psalm 37:7-9 (TLB)* □_____ □_____

3. Don't take it on yourself to repay a wrong. Trust the Lord and he will make it right. *Proverbs 20:22 (TEV)* □_____ □_____

4. Blessed are you when people insult you, persecute you and falsely say all kinds of evil against you because of me. Rejoice and be glad, because great is your reward in heaven, for in the same way they persecuted the prophets who were before you. *Matthew 5:11-12 (NIV)* □_____ □_____

I have such a doormat personality. Does God want me to be more assertive?

1. Who gives man his mouth? Who makes him deaf or dumb? Who gives him sight or makes him blind? It is I, the Lord. Now, go! I will help you to speak, and I will tell you what to say. *Exodus 4:11-12 (TEV)* □_____ □_____

2. When I called, you answered me; you made me bold and stouthearted. *Psalm 138:3 (NIV)* □_____ □_____

3. "My grace is all you need; for my power is strongest when you are weak." I am most happy, then, to be proud of my weaknesses, in order to feel the protection of Christ's power over me. *2 Corinthians 12:9 (TEV)* □_____ □_____

4. May you be made strong with all the strength which comes from his glorious might, so that you may be able to endure everything with patience. *Colossians 1:11 (TEV)* □_____ □_____

5. Reverence for the Lord gives confidence and security to a man and his family. *Proverbs 14:26 (TEV)*

□ _____ □ _____

I wish I were not shy. Will God help me to be brave?

1. For the Holy Spirit, God's gift, does not want you to be afraid of people, but to be wise and strong, and to love them and enjoy being with them. *2 Timothy 1:7 (TLB)*

□ _____ □ _____

2. We can confidently say, "The Lord is my helper, I will not be afraid; what can man do to me?" *Hebrews 13:6 (RSV)* □ _____ □ _____

3. I can do everything through him who gives me strength. *Philippians 4:13 (NIV)*

□ _____ □ _____

4. Do not fear, for I am with you; do not anxiously look about you, for I am your God. I will strengthen you, surely I will help you, surely I will uphold you with My righteous right hand. *Isaiah 41:10 (NASB)*

□ _____ □ _____

People always seem to let me down. Can I trust God to be true to me?

1. Even when we are too weak to have any faith left, he remains faithful to us and will help us, for he cannot disown us who are part of himself, and he will always carry out his promises to us. *2 Timothy 2:13 (TLB)*

□ _____ □ _____

2. Know therefore that the Lord your God is God; he is the faithful God, keeping his covenant of love to a thousand generations of those who love him and keep his commands. *Deuteronomy 7:9 (NIV)*

□_____ □_____

3. For no matter how many promises God has made, they are "Yes" in Christ. And so through him the "Amen" is spoken by us to the glory of God. Now it is God who makes . . . us . . . stand firm in Christ. He anointed us, set his seal of ownership on us, and put his Spirit in our hearts as a deposit, guaranteeing what is to come. *2 Corinthians 1:20-22 (NIV)*

□_____ □_____

4. I am not going to leave you alone in the world—I am coming to you. *John 14:18 (Phillips)*

□_____ □_____

5. For I am certain that nothing can separate us from his love: neither death nor life; neither angels nor other heavenly rulers or powers; neither the present nor the future; neither the world above nor the world below— there is nothing in all creation that will ever be able to separate us from the love of God which is ours through Christ Jesus our Lord. *Romans 8:38-39 (TEV)*

□_____ □_____

I'm involved in a homosexual relationship. Will God help me out of this trap?

1. Sexual sin is never right: our bodies were not made for that, but for the Lord, and the Lord wants to fill our bodies with himself. *1 Corinthians 6:13 (TLB)*

□_____ □_____

2. No temptation has come your way that is too hard for flesh and blood to bear. But God can be trusted not to allow you to suffer any temptation beyond your powers of endurance. He will see to it that every temptation has its way out, so that it will be possible for you to bear it. *1 Corinthians 10:13 (Phillips)*

☐ _____ ☐ _____

3. Don't you know that the wicked will not inherit the kingdom of God? Do not be deceived: Neither the sexually immoral nor idolaters nor adulterers nor male prostitutes nor homosexual offenders nor thieves nor the greedy nor drunkards nor slanderers nor swindlers will inherit the kingdom of God. And that is what some of you were. But you were washed, you were sanctified, you were justified in the name of the Lord Jesus Christ and by the Spirit of our God. *1 Corinthians 6:9–11 (NIV)*

☐ _____ ☐ _____

4. Submit yourselves, then, to God. Resist the devil, and he will flee from you. *James 4:7 (NIV)*

☐ _____ ☐ _____

My boyfriend/girlfriend has just broken up with me and I'm absolutely devastated. Will God help me through this pain and fill the emptiness in my heart?

1. The Lord is near to the brokenhearted, and saves those who are crushed in spirit. *Psalm 34:18 (NASB)*

☐ _____ ☐ _____

2. The Lord will surely comfort Zion and will look with compassion on all her ruins; he will make her deserts like Eden, her wastelands like the garden of the Lord. Joy and gladness will be found in her, thanksgiving and the sound of singing. *Isaiah 51:3 (NIV)*

☐ _____ ☐ _____

3. Praise be to the God and Father of our Lord Jesus Christ, the Father of compassion and the God of all comfort, who comforts us in all our troubles, so that we can comfort those in any trouble with the comfort we ourselves have received from God. *2 Corinthians 1:3-4 (NIV)* □_____ □_____

4. You have changed my sadness into a joyful dance; you have taken away my sorrow and surrounded me with joy. So I will not be silent; I will sing praise to you. Lord, you are my God; I will give you thanks forever. *Psalm 30:11-12 (TEV)*

□_____ □_____

5. Seek your happiness in the Lord, and he will give you your heart's desire. *Psalm 37:4 (TEV)*

□_____ □_____

My friend has hurt me deeply. Will God show me how to forgive?

1. This is how we know what love is: Jesus Christ laid down his life for us. And we ought to lay down our lives for our brothers. *1 John 3:16 (NIV)*

□_____ □_____

2. Get rid of all bitterness, passion, and anger. No more shouting or insults. No more hateful feelings of any sort. Instead, be kind and tender-hearted to one another, and forgive one another, as God has forgiven you in Christ. *Ephesians 4:31-32 (TEV)*

□_____ □_____

3. Be gentle and ready to forgive; never hold grudges. Remember, the Lord forgave you, so you must forgive others. *Colossians 3:13 (TLB)*

□_____ □_____

4. But if your brother wrongs you, go and have it out with him at once—just between the two of you. If he will listen to you, you have won him back as your brother. *Matthew 18:15 (Phillips)*

□_____ □_____

Some people really bug me. Can I count on God to give me more patience?

1. May God who gives patience, steadiness, and encouragement help you to live in complete harmony with each other—each with the attitude of Christ toward the other. And then all of us can praise the Lord together with one voice, giving glory to God, the Father of our Lord Jesus Christ. *Romans 15:5-6 (TLB)*

☐_____ ☐_____

2. But when the Holy Spirit controls our lives he will produce this kind of fruit in us: love, joy, peace, patience, kindness, goodness, faithfulness, gentleness and self-control. *Galatians 5:22 (TLB)*

☐_____ ☐_____

3. The Lord's servant must not quarrel. He must be kind toward all, a good and patient teacher, who is gentle as he corrects his opponents. It may be that God will give them the opportunity to repent and come to know the truth. *2 Timothy 2:24-25 (TEV)*

☐_____ ☐_____

4. Be humble and gentle. Be patient with each other, making allowance for each other's faults because of your love. Try always to be led along together by the Holy Spirit, and so be at peace with one another. *Ephesians 4:2-3 (TLB)* ☐_____ ☐_____

It's hard for me not to hate someone who has taken my place in someone else's life. Will God help me with my jealousy?

1. The Spirit has given us life; he must also control our lives. We must not be proud, or irritate one another, or be jealous of one another. *Galatians 5:25-26 (TEV)*

☐_____ ☐_____

2. This love of which I speak is slow to lose patience—it looks for a way of being constructive. It is not possessive: it is neither anxious to impress nor does it cherish inflated ideas of its own importance. *1 Corinthians 13:4 (Phillips)* ☐_____ ☐_____

3. Let each of you look not only to his own interests, but also to the interests of others. *Philippians 2:4 (RSV)*
☐_____ ☐_____

4. Love must be sincere. Hate what is evil; cling to what is good. Be devoted to one another in brotherly love. Honor one another above yourselves. *Romans 12:9-10 (NIV)* ☐_____ ☐_____

5. A relaxed attitude lengthens a man's life; jealousy rots it away. *Proverbs 14:30 (TLB)*
☐_____ ☐_____

I want to share my faith with others. How can I be more than a "witless witness"?

1. But you will be filled with power when the Holy Spirit comes on you, and you will be witnesses for me in Jerusalem, in all of Judea and Samaria, and to the ends of the earth. *Acts 1:8 (TEV)*
☐_____ ☐_____

2. Therefore go and make disciples of all nations, baptizing them in the name of the Father and of the Son and of the Holy Spirit, and teaching them to obey everything I have commanded you. And surely I will be with you always, to the very end of the age. *Matthew 28:19-20 (NIV)* ☐_____ ☐_____

3. Since we know that his new glory will never go away, we can preach with great boldness. *2 Corinthians 3:12 (TLB)* ☐_____ ☐_____

4. When they deliver you up, do not be anxious how you are to speak or what you are to say; for what you are to say will be given to you in that hour; for it is not you who speak, but the Spirit of your Father speaking through you. *Matthew 10:19–20 (RSV)*

☐ _____ ☐ _____

I get enraged at bigots. Can God keep me from being bigotted about bigots?

1. We who are strong ought to bear with the failings of the weak. *Romans 15:1 (RSV)*

☐ _____ ☐ _____

2. Therefore, as God's chosen people, holy and dearly loved, clothe yourselves with compassion, kindness, humility, gentleness and patience. Bear with each other and forgive whatever grievances you may have against one another. Forgive as the Lord forgave you. And over all these virtues put on love, which binds them together in perfect unity. *Colossians 3:12–14 (NIV)*

☐ _____ ☐ _____

3. And all of you serve each other with humble spirits, for God gives special blessings to those who are humble, but sets himself against those who are proud. If you will humble yourselves under the mighty hand of God, in his good time he will lift you up. *1 Peter 5:5–6 (TLB)*

☐ _____ ☐ _____

Many people have less than I do, but if I give to them, how will I have enough left for myself?

1. Give to others, and God will give to you: you will receive a full measure, a generous helping, poured into your hands—all that you can hold. The measure you use for others is the one God will use for you. *Luke 6:38 (TEV)* □_____ □_____

2. God will give you much so that you can give away much, and when we take your gifts to those who need them they will break out into thanksgiving and praise to God for your help. *2 Corinthians 9:11 (TLB)*
□_____ □_____

3. Be generous, and you will be prosperous. Help others, and you will be helped. *Proverbs 11:25 (TEV)*
□_____ □_____

4. Bring the whole tithe into the storehouse, that there may be food in my house. Test me in this, says the Lord Almighty, and see if I will not throw open the floodgates of heaven and pour out so much blessing that you will not have room enough for it. *Malachi 3:10 (NIV)*
□_____ □_____

5. God is not unjust; he will not forget your work and the love you have shown him as you have helped his people and continue to help them. *Hebrews 6:10 (NIV)*
□_____ □_____

My Life at School

I wanted to do so well this term and I've already blown the first test. Can God give me the energy to keep trying?

1. Be strong—not in yourselves but in the Lord, in the power of his boundless strength. *Ephesians 6:10 (Phillips)*
☐_____ ☐_____

2. He strengthens those who are weak and tired. Those who trust in the Lord for help will find their strength renewed. They will rise on wings like eagles; they will run and not get weary; they will walk and not grow weak. *Isaiah 40:29, 31 (TEV)*
☐_____ ☐_____

3. Whatever you do, work at it with all your heart, as working for the Lord, not for me, since you know that you will receive an inheritance from the Lord as a reward. It is the Lord Christ you are serving. *Colossians 3:23–24 (NIV)* ☐_____ ☐_____

4. I will always guide you and satisfy you with good things. I will keep you strong and well. You will be like a garden that has plenty of water, like a spring of water that never goes dry. *Isaiah 58:11 (TEV)*
☐_____ ☐_____

I just received a D on my test and I'm really hurting. How do I measure up in God's eyes?

1. The Father himself loves you because you have loved me and have believed that I came from God. *John 16:27 (NIV)* ☐_____ ☐_____

2. So now, since we have been made right in God's sight by faith in his promises, we can have real peace with him because of what Jesus Christ our Lord has done for us. For because of our faith, he has brought us into this place of highest privilege where we now stand, and we confidently and joyfully look forward to actually becoming all that God has had in mind for us to be. *Romans 5:1-2 (TLB)* ☐_____ ☐_____

3. I am poor and needy, yet the Lord is thinking about me right now! O my God, you are my helper. You are my Savior. *Psalm 40:17 (TLB)*
☐_____ ☐_____

4. The Lord your God is with you; his power gives you victory. The Lord will take delight in you, and in his love he will give you new life. He will sing and be joyful over you. *Zephaniah 3:17 (TEV)*
☐_____ ☐_____

I'm so busy and there are so many demands on my time, I don't even have time to think. How can I slow down?

1. Don't worry about anything; instead, pray about everything; tell God your needs and don't forget to thank him for his answers. If you do this you will experience God's peace, which is far more wonderful than the human mind can understand. His peace will keep your thoughts and your hearts quiet and at rest as you trust in Christ Jesus. *Philippians 4:6-7 (TLB)*
☐_____ ☐_____

2. You will keep in perfect peace him whose mind is steadfast, because he trusts in you. *Isaiah 26:3 (NIV)*
☐_____ ☐_____

3. Come to me, all of you who are weary and overburdened, and I will give you rest! *Matthew 11:28 (Phillips)* ☐_____ ☐_____

4. Cease striving and know that I am God; I will be exalted among the nations, I will be exalted in the earth. *Psalm 46:10 (NASB)*

□_____ □_____

5. Be still before the Lord, and wait patiently for him. *Psalm 37:7 (RSV)* □_____ □_____

6. In repentance and rest you shall be saved, in quietness and trust is your strength. *Isaiah 30:15 (NASB)*

□_____ □_____

Some of my teachers are sarcastic and critical of my performance. Is God critical and judgmental too?

1. The Lord is merciful and loving, slow to become angry and full of constant love. He does not punish us as we deserve or repay us for our sins and wrongs. *Psalm 103:8, 10 (TEV)* □_____ □_____

2. Who would dare to accuse us, whom God has chosen? God himself has declared us free from sin. Who is in a position to condemn? Only Christ Jesus, and Christ died for us, Christ also rose for us, Christ reigns in power for us, Christ prays for us! *Romans 8:33–34 (Phillips)*

□_____ □_____

3. But now thus says the Lord, he who created you, O Jacob, he who formed you, O Israel: "Fear not, for I have redeemed you; I have called you by name, you are mine." *Isaiah 43:1 (RSV)*

□_____ □_____

4. He will keep you steadfast in the faith to the end, so that when his day comes you need fear no condemnation. God is utterly dependable, and it is he who has called you into fellowship with his Son Jesus Christ, our Lord. *1 Corinthians 1:8–9 (Phillips)*

□_____ □_____

I wish I could drop out of school. Would God love me even if I were a dropout?

1. I have loved you with an everlasting love; therefore I have continued my faithfulness to you. *Jeremiah 31:3 (RSV)* ☐_____ ☐_____

2. I alone know the plans I have for you, plans to bring you prosperity and not disaster, plans to bring about the future you hope for. *Jeremiah 29:11 (TEV)*
☐_____ ☐_____

3. For it is by grace that you are saved, through faith. This does not depend on anything you have achieved, it is the free gift of God; and because it is not earned no man can boast about it. *Ephesians 2:8-9 (Phillips)*
☐_____ ☐_____

4. Just as a father has compassion on his children, so the Lord has compassion on those who fear Him. For He Himself knows our frame; He is mindful that we are but dust. *Psalm 103:13-14 (NASB)*
☐_____ ☐_____

It's scary to be out on my own for the first time. How can I be sure that God is still with me?

1. It is the Lord who goes before you; he will be with you, he will not fail you or forsake you; do not fear or be dismayed. *Deuteronomy 31:8 (RSV)*
☐_____ ☐_____

2. My help will come from the Lord, who made heaven and earth. He will not let you fall; your protector is always awake. The protector of Israel never dozes or sleeps. The Lord will guard you; he is by your side to protect you. The Lord will protect you from all danger; he will keep you safe. He will protect you as you come and go now and forever. *Psalm 121:2-5, 7-8 (TEV)*

☐_____ ☐_____

3. I am not going to leave you alone in the world—I am coming to you. *John 14:18 (Phillips)*

☐_____ ☐_____

4. For this God is our God for ever and ever; he will be our guide even to the end. *Psalm 48:14 (NIV)*

☐_____ ☐_____

I feel so stupid and thick-brained. Does God really love slow people and under-achievers like me?

1. The Lord is faithful to all his promises and loving towards all he has made. The Lord upholds all those who fall and lifts up all who are bowed down. *Psalm 145:13-14 (NIV)* ☐_____ ☐_____

2. For you created my inmost being; you knit me together in my mother's womb. I praise you because I am fearfully and wonderfully made; your works are wonderful, I know that full well. *Psalm 139:13-14 (NIV)*

☐_____ ☐_____

3. May our Lord Jesus Christ himself and God our Father (who has loved us and given us unending encouragement and unfailing hope by his grace) inspire you with courage and confidence in every good thing you say or do. *2 Thessalonians 2:16-17 (Phillips)*

☐_____ ☐_____

4. He has by his own action given us everything that is necessary for living the truly good life, in allowing us to know the one who has called us to him, through his own glorious goodness. *2 Peter 1:3 (Phillips)*

☐_____ ☐_____

87

I'm terrified of flunking out of school. How can I deal with my anxiety?

1. Don't worry over anything whatever; whenever you pray tell God every detail of your needs in thankful prayer, and the peace of God, which surpasses human understanding, will keep constant guard over your hearts and minds as they rest in Christ Jesus. *Philippians 4:6-7 (Phillips)* □_____ □_____

2. Let him have all your worries and cares, for he is always thinking about you and watching everything that concerns you. *1 Peter 5:7 (TLB)*
□_____ □_____

3. Now glory be to God who by his mighty power at work within us is able to do far more than we would ever dare to ask or even dream of—infinitely beyond our highest prayers, desires, thoughts, or hopes. *Ephesians 3:20 (TLB)* □_____ □_____

4. In me you may have peace. In this world you will have trouble. But take heart! I have overcome the world. *John 16:33 (NIV)* □_____ □_____

I got straight A's this semester. How can God help me to keep my priorities straight and keep me from pride?

1. We should remember that while this "knowing" may make a man look big, it is only love that can make him grow to his full stature. For if a man thinks he "knows" he may still be quite ignorant of what he ought to know. But if he loves God he is the man who is known to God. *1 Corinthians 8:1-3 (Phillips)*
□_____ □_____

2. As God's messenger I give each of you God's warning: Be honest in your estimate of yourselves, measuring

your value by how much faith God has given you.
Romans 12:3 (TLB)

☐ _____ ☐ _____

3. But every good endowment and every complete gift must come from above, from the Father of all lights, with whom there is never the slightest variation or shadow of inconsistency. *James 1:17 (Phillips)*

☐ _____ ☐ _____

The person who sits next to me cheats in every exam and then gets A's. Will God help me to avoid being bitter about this situation?

1. Pray much for others; plead for God's mercy upon them; give thanks for all he is going to do for them. *1 Timothy 2:1 (TLB)*

☐ _____ ☐ _____

2. Put on then, as God's chosen ones, holy and beloved, compassion, kindness, lowliness, meekness, and patience, forbearing one another and, if one has a complaint against another, forgiving each other; as the Lord has forgiven you, so you also must forgive. And above all these put on love, which binds everything together in perfect harmony. *Colossians 3:12–14 (RSV)*

☐ _____ ☐ _____

3. Let it be your ambition to live at peace with all men and to achieve holiness "without which no man shall see the Lord." Be careful that none of you fails to respond to the grace of God, for if he does there can spring up in him a bitter spirit which can poison the lives of many others. *Hebrews 12:14–15 (Phillips)*

☐ _____ ☐ _____

Prayer Page

date	prayer

date	prayer

date	prayer

date   **prayer**

_____

_____

_____

_____

_____

date   **prayer**

_____

_____

_____

_____

_____

date   **prayer**

_____

_____

_____

_____

date   prayer

_____

_____

_____

_____

date   prayer

_____

_____

_____

_____

date   prayer

_____

_____

_____

_____

date   **prayer**

_____

_____

_____

_____

_____

date   **prayer**

_____

_____

_____

_____

_____

date   **prayer**

_____

_____

_____

_____

_____

date   **prayer**

_____

_____

_____

_____

date   **prayer**

_____

_____

_____

_____

date   **prayer**

_____

_____

_____

_____

date   **prayer**

_____

_____

_____

_____

date   **prayer**

_____

_____

_____

_____

date   **prayer**

_____

_____

_____

_____

date **prayer**

_____

_____

_____

_____

date **prayer**

_____

_____

_____

_____

date **prayer**

_____

_____

_____

_____